# Get **Clients NOW!**™

**Get Clients NOW!**
by C.J. Hayden, MCC

(877) 946-4722 toll free
(415) 981-8845 outside US

info@getclientsnow.com

*Subscribe to my
free e-mail newsletter!*
**www.getclientsnow.com**

*To your
marketing success!*

# Get **Clients NOW!**™

## A 28-Day Marketing Program for Professionals and Consultants

C.J. Hayden

## AMACOM

American Management Association International

New York ■ Atlanta ■ Boston ■ Chicago ■ Kansas City ■ San Francisco
Washington, D.C. ■ Brussels ■ Mexico City ■ Tokyo ■ Toronto

This book is available at a special discount
when ordered in bulk quantities.
For information, contact Special Sales Department,
AMACOM, an imprint of AMA Publications,
a division of American Management Association
International, 1601 Broadway, New York, NY 10019.

Get Clients Now!™ is a trademark of C.J. Hayden, San Fransisco, Calif.

Library of Congress Cataloging-in-Publication Data

Hayden, C.J.
    Get clients now!™ : a 28-day market program for professionals and consultants/C.J. Hayden.
      p.    cm.
    Includes index
    ISBN 0-8144-7992-8
    1.  Marketing—Study and teaching.   I.  Title.
    HF5415.H296   1999
    658.8—dc21                       98–41140
                                          CIP

Printing number

10

To my clients, who taught me all I know.

# Contents

# Foreword

I bet I can read your mind. Let's see . . .

You're holding this book. (That much is obvious.) You're thinking about reading it. (Or you wouldn't be holding it.) But you're wondering if it's for you. (Right?)

Well, here's an easy way to discover if you should take the time to read this book. Just take this simple quiz and see for yourself:

1. Do you know where to begin to find new clients?
2. Do you have a strategy to follow to reach your goals?
3. Do you stay motivated every day, no matter what happens?

If you answered no to any or all of the above, you need this book today. How will it help? Get Clients Now! is a 28-day program for sales and marketing success that gives you a step-by-step action plan for getting all the clients you need. It tells you what to do first, how to meet your goals with the least amount of time and effort, and how to keep yourself motivated as you go.

Need I say more?

Truth is, virtually everyone in business is ignorant of how to get new business. The most common question people ask me is, "How do I get clients?" When I ask them what they are doing to find clients, they usually shrug. The average person in business has no idea how to get and keep new clients—let alone how to do it in 28 days. The average person simply runs a small ad, hands out flyers, goes to meetings, or maybe sends out a news release. But the average person in business goes bankrupt within three years!

Thank goodness for C.J. and this incredible program. Now whenever someone asks me that popular question, I'll just hand them this book. I'm impressed with the simplicity of the cookbook-to-success approach this book takes. Each day is mapped out to make the doing a snap. With this tool at your side, handling the three questions I posed will be a breeze: You'll know where to start, you'll have your strategy, and you'll have your motivation. What could be easier?

I think your decision is clear: Take this book home with you. Read it. Then use it. As a result, by this time next month you'll have new clients, new profits, and a big smile on your face.

And you certainly won't be average.

Joe "Mr. Fire!" Vitale, marketing specialist and author
of seven books, including *There's a Customer Born
Every Minute: P. T. Barnum's Secrets to Business
Success* (AMACOM, 1998), www.mrfire.com

# Acknowledgments

I wish to extend my heartfelt thanks to the following people for their generous assistance in the creation of this book: the coaches, consultants, and authors who contributed their time and words of wisdom; my agent, Sheryl Fullerton, whose patience and perseverance kept this project alive; Barbara McDonald of Native Design for her superb illustrations; my mentor, Laura Whitworth, who gave me the idea for the program that led to this book; marketing gurus Jay Conrad Levinson and Joe Vitale for their kind encouragement and invaluable inspiration; my sister coaches who supported me in countless ways while this book was being written: Breeze Carlile, Margo Komenar, Caterina Rando, Shannon Seek, and Cat Williford; and the makers of Clif Bar, whose fine product fueled many late nights of writing.

C.J. Hayden

# Introduction

*The significant problems we face cannot be solved at the level of thinking that created them.*

—Albert Einstein

If you are ready to get clients *now*, you have come to the right place. Get Clients Now! is a complete marketing and sales system for professionals, consultants, and anyone else who markets a service business. This book contains a 28-day program for sales and marketing success. It has all the tools you need to get your marketing efforts unstuck, make an effective action plan, and start getting clients.

It's easy to think that there is some hidden secret to successful marketing and sales. When you consider all of the books you could read, seminars you could take, or consultants you could hire, it makes the process of learning how to market yourself seem huge, mysterious, or even terrifying. But in fact there is a simple answer to all your marketing and sales problems, and it's right here in this book. *The magic formula for service business marketing and sales is choosing a set of simple, effective things to do, and doing them consistently.* The Get Clients Now! system will enable you to do just that.

Get Clients Now! uses a cookbook model to help you create a sales and marketing action plan. First, you will discover the success ingredients that are missing from your current marketing and sales activities. Then you will choose from the Action Plan Menu the specific courses of action you should take. Detailed recipes for the recommended tactics and tools are provided to help you successfully implement your plan.

Once your action plan is designed, the 28-day program will put your ideas into action immediately. Many people who have used the program report improved results within just a few days. You can use the program quite successfully by yourself; to make it even more powerful, team up with a business buddy, with an action group, or with a personal coach (see Chapter 3 for more details).

To make the most effective use of this book, read Chapters 1 through 5 in order, completing the exercises as you go. When you are ready to begin the 28-day program, start reading Chapter 6, one section per day. Two rest days per week are built into the program. Chapters 7 through 10 contain a collection of marketing "recipes" that you can use for reference while you are designing your action plan or for marketing ideas and inspiration at any time. Each of these chapters covers one stage of the universal marketing cycle you will learn about in Chapter 2, where you will choose one stage to work on during the program. You will need to look at only the chapter that pertains to the stage you select.

Throughout the book, you will find suggestions, stories, and tips from sales and marketing experts, business and personal coaches, and others familiar with the Get Clients Now! program. Whenever possible, web site addresses have been included for these people. If you visit these sites, you will find a wealth of additional resources to help you increase your success at sales and marketing.

If you have questions about the program that go beyond the book or for extra advice and inspiration about service business marketing, visit www. GetClientsNow.com.

The Get Clients Now! system is entirely reusable. After completing the program once, you can use the same action plan for another 28 days, or begin again with Chapter 2 to design a revised plan. Either way, you will continue to benefit from the focus, direction, and motivation that the system provides.

> Here is Edward Bear coming downstairs now, bump, bump, bump on the back of his head behind Christopher Robin. It is, as far as he knows, the only way of coming down stairs, but sometimes he feels that there really is another way, if only he could stop bumping for a moment and think of it.
>
> —A. A. Milne, *Winnie-the-Pooh*

# Part I

## The Setup

# Chapter 1

# What Really Works? Effective Marketing Strategies

*If you have built castles in the air, your work need not be lost; that is
where they should be. Now put the foundations under them.*

—Henry David Thoreau

## Marketing Made Simple

Marketing is telling people what you do . . . over and over. There are many
ways of telling people—in person, in writing, through the media, by phone—
but you do have to *tell* them. You can't just wait for the phone to start ringing.
You have to tell them over and over. According to market positioning expert
Jack Trout, the average American is exposed to 4,000 marketing messages per
day. Where is your message in all that communication? What will make others remember you if they hear about you only once?

Getting prospective clients to hear what you have to offer and remember
you until they need your service can seem like an enormous challenge. So how
do people in your line of work—professional services, consulting, and other
service businesses—get clients? Ask any successful businessperson that question, and this is what you will hear: "Referrals." "Networking." "Making contacts and following up." "Word of mouth."

It's simple stuff; you probably already knew the answers. So why don't
you have all the clients you need? If you're like most other first-time users of
the Get Clients Now! system, one or all of the following reasons will sound
familiar:

*Barriers to Success*

• *You can't decide where to begin.* Marketing your business seems
like an overwhelming project. There are so many ideas to consider and

so many choices to make, and you want to make sure you are doing it right. So you worry about how best to spend your time and money. Struck by "analysis paralysis," you start and stop, sit and stew, or just do nothing.

• *You aren't sure how to put the pieces together.* You know you should be making cold calls but think maybe you need to finish that new brochure first. You suspect it might be time to develop some new leads, but what about those follow-up calls you've been meaning to make? You wonder if all the networking will ever pay off, and whether that speaking engagement will really generate any clients. You don't have a system, a program, or a plan.

• *You can't stay motivated.* Even when you know exactly what you need to do, often you just don't do it. With no boss looking over your shoulder, it's too easy to avoid marketing and sales. When you don't see immediate results, you get discouraged. When someone rejects your sales pitch, it's hard not to take it personally. It's so tempting just to wait for the phone to ring, and blame your lack of business on the economy, the weather, or the time of year.

If you have ever had these thoughts or others like them, you are not alone. People who market service businesses rarely fail due to lack of information about effective sales and marketing techniques. They fail because they don't use the information that is right at their fingertips. The reason the Get Clients Now! system works is that it eliminates the three barriers listed above, so you can take immediate action.

### How the System Works

• *It breaks down the marketing and sales process into a series of simple steps* so you will know exactly where to begin to get clients today.

• *It organizes the steps into a tested process built around three powerful components: motivation, direction, and evidence.* The system shows how all the pieces of the sales and marketing puzzle fit together: what to do, when to do it, and how to measure your results.

• *It provides a motivational coach-yourself-to-success 28-day program* packed with tools and techniques to help you overcome fear, resistance, procrastination, and other barriers to effective action.

In order for you to use the system successfully, you don't need to know much more about sales and marketing than you do right now. You have already learned the most important secret: that you need a system in the first place. But there are a few  concepts that will help you make the best choices about what to include in your own personal program, and that's what the rest of this chapter is about.

"There are hundreds of ways to market yourself," maintains Rich Fettke, a business and personal success coach, and past president of the Professional and Personal Coaches Association. "You can create a promo kit to send the media, speak at business groups and functions, send out monthly postcards, e-mails, and faxes. You can call people on the phone and personally deliver your unique marketing message.

"You can do any of these things, but will you? You can't do all of them at the same time. The trick to great marketing is to get the same people to hear about you over and over. The only way to do this without being overwhelmed and frustrated is to create a sales and marketing plan and then stick with it. Your plan needs to be specific, measurable, and attainable (with some risk), and include goal dates and deadlines. Setting up daily success habits for yourself will also lead you toward accomplishing your goals, step by step."

Rich has chosen to use the Get Clients Now! system with his clients "because it gives them an easy-to-follow structure for attracting more business. It gets them into action, and action creates results."

Rich Fettke, Certified Professional and Personal Coach,
Fettke Group, www.fettke.com

## What Works and What Doesn't?

In the Introduction, you learned the first secret of successful service business marketing: Choose a set of simple, effective things to do, and do them consistently. Here is the second secret: *Marketing a service business is not the same as marketing a product.* Products are tangible; you can see them, touch them, maybe even taste them before you buy. Services are intangible. You can't see them until they are demonstrated. They can't be touched or tasted. Because a service is intangible, until it is performed for you, you have no idea how it will turn out, whether you will like it, or whether it will work for your problem, situation, or opportunity.

Therefore, when you purchase a service for the first time, you must rely on your judgment about the person or organization delivering it. There is an old saying in sales and marketing: "People do business with people they know, like, and trust." If a potential customer gets to know you, learns to like you, and believes that he or she can trust you, you probably have a sale. Without your having at least one of those factors in place, getting the business will be an almost impossible task.

Keep this crucial rule in mind as you look at Figure 1-1, which depicts marketing strategies for the service business. This diagram operates on three levels simultaneously. First, it shows the six sales and marketing strategies that service providers can use. Second, it rates the strategies in order of effectiveness, from direct contact at the top to advertising at the bottom. We'll look at each of these strategies in more detail in the next section, but notice that there is a strong connection between effectiveness and the know-like-and-trust factor. Strategies 1 through 3 are much more likely to create a personal relationship between you and the buyer than strategies 4 through 6. The relative order of the individual strategies is unimportant, but the overall ranking is critical to making the right choices about marketing. Direct contact and follow-up almost always works, but advertising alone almost never does.

The effectiveness of a particular strategy can vary with the situation. A psychotherapist, for example, might find that direct contact and follow-up with potential clients would be inappropriate, and therefore rely more on networking and referral building. A poor public speaker would do well to avoid that strategy and concentrate on writing and publicity instead.

The third level of information shown in Figure 1-1 is the impact that each strategy creates: outreach, visibility, and/or credibility. Knowing the impact of a strategy will also help you determine whether to use it. Direct contact and follow-up is an outreach strategy, and networking and referral building is both an outreach and a visibility strategy. Public speaking and writing and publicity have the impact of both visibility and credibility, and promotional events and advertising have only the visibility impact.

Notice also that the impacts themselves have an effectiveness ranking. Outreach strategies are clearly the most effective, and visibility-only strategies the least. Strategies that combine visibility with outreach or credibility are ranked in the middle.

## What Goes Into a Strategy?

Think of marketing strategies as the highest-level organizing principle for your marketing and sales activities. When you are trying to decide if you should spend more effort on networking or publicity, for example, remember that networking is ranked as more effective. If you are wondering whether to plunk down a large sum of money for an ad special, ask first what that money would buy if you spent it on promoting yourself as a public speaker.

Every strategy is made up of one or more tactics, or, to put it another way, you use specific tactics to execute a chosen strategy. After the definition of each strategy in the following sections is a list of tactics you might use to employ it. And Part III of this book contains detailed marketing recipes that will tell you just how to use these tactics.

**Figure 1-1. Marketing strategies for the service business.**

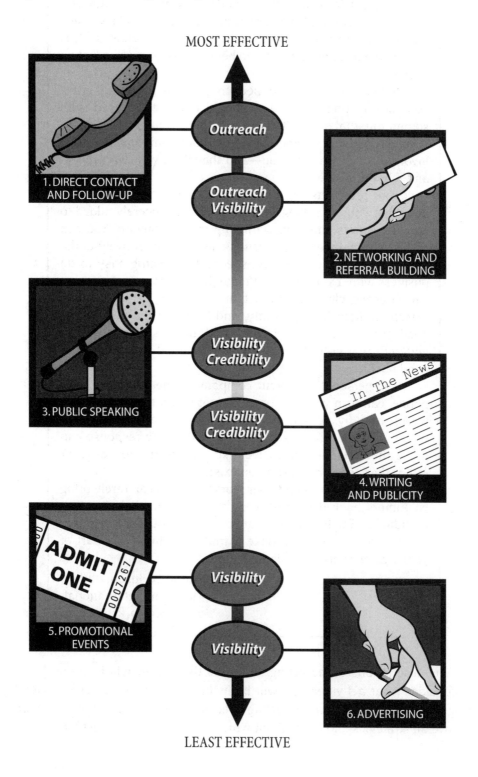

"The highest form of public relations is human relations," declares Jay Conrad Levinson, author of the Guerrilla Marketing series of books. "People like to buy from friends, so it is crucial to make the human bond before you can make a lasting business bond.

"If you can't see the connection, perhaps marketing is not your strong point, and you should become involved with something that doesn't involve human beings! The more humanity prospects experience from your company, the more involved they'll be with you—and they'll prove it with repeat and referral business.

"Your prospects are going to have to buy you before they buy what you are selling. Humanity that is sincerely added to a cold business situation warms up the transaction. You can add humanity by asking questions, listening attentively to the answers, respecting your prospect's time, being easy to do business with. Don't underestimate the importance of a warm, sincere smile, clear eye contact, and using the person's name. It feels human, it feels comfy, and it makes the person feel good. When the customer feels good, the customer connects you with that good feeling. That's why good feelings lead to good business.

"The personality of your company, as heard on the telephone, can turn your customers on, or it can turn them off. A warm, friendly person answering the phone can lead to a warm, friendly relationship. A cold, unfriendly response can make the caller feel intrusive, like an interruption of work rather than the very reason you exist.

"No matter how good your marketing is, it can rarely bring customers back if they were disappointed in their first go-round with you. It can't generate profits for you if your word of mouth works against it. Make warmth and humanity part of your written marketing plan."

Jay Conrad Levinson, author,
Guerrilla Marketing International,
www.gmarketing.com

The descriptions of marketing strategies that follow will help you begin to consider what activities you will be including in your Get Clients Now! program. Don't worry about selecting specific tactics at this point. Focus on the overall strategies and think about which ones might work best for you.

**Direct Contact and Follow-Up**

*Direct contact* means making personal contact with a prospective customer by phone, in person, or by mail, fax, or e-mail. To get results, your first contact must be personal—not a form letter or a broadcast. If you make contact in writing, personalize your communication by addressing it to a specific person and mentioning some issue you know he or she is facing. If you don't do this, you are merely generating direct mail, which is an advertising strategy.

After your initial contact, more impersonal communications, like mailings and newsletters, can become effective follow-up techniques. But for interested prospects, use these tactics as a supplement to follow-up calls, not a substitute for them.

Note that the marketing strategy of direct contact and follow-up refers to contact with a prospective client. It does not refer to the contact and follow-up activities you may do with colleagues and others while you are using the strategy of networking and referral building.

### Tactics for Direct Contact and Follow-Up

• *Cold calling.* Call a complete stranger on the phone. Works best if you have reason to believe the person needs your service and you can tell her why with no information from her.

• *Warm calling.* Call someone you have some connection with—someone you have met before, someone who has been referred to you, or someone who belongs to the same association as you do.

• *Canvassing.* Walk into an office (or several) without an appointment, or even without a contact. Works better for information gathering than for actually selling.

• *Lunch or coffee (with prospects).* An excellent follow-up strategy when your services are expensive or difficult to explain, or the sales cycle is long.

• *In-person appointments.* What many people do to present their service in detail. May lead to a proposal or directly to a sale.

• *"Accidental" meetings.* When you can't seem to reach someone you know would be interested in your service if only you could talk to him, try to "run into him" at a meeting or seminar.

• *Personal letters.* Send a personal letter to a hot prospect. This is extremely effective when it is truly personal, not just boilerplate, and is coupled with a follow-up phone call.

- *Announcement card or letter.* If you are just starting out, this is a great way to let everyone know what you're doing. Follow up with phone calls.

- *Nice-to-meet-you notes.* When you meet someone and collect her business card, send a note. Include literature if it seems appropriate. Follow up further if you like.

- *Sending clippings or cartoons.* In a nonthreatening way, keep in touch with people you've met by sending clippings or cartoons they will enjoy.

- *Extending invitations.* Invite prospects or contacts to a meeting or seminar you are planning to go to anyway. It's an excuse to contact them without selling.

- *Reminder cards.* When your list of contacts becomes large, do a mailing to remind people you're around. Cards can be easier than writing a newsletter, and postcards are cheaper to mail.

- *Newsletters.* An effective follow-up technique when your service provides valuable information. Use print or e-mail newsletters to show off your expertise and remind people you're available.

 **Networking and Referral Building**

Don't limit your picture of what networking means to circulating through a room exchanging business cards. A broader view of networking is creating a pool of contacts from which you can draw clients, referrals, resources, ideas, and information. When you go to a networking event, you may meet prospective customers, but you will also make other valuable contacts. Just as you would follow up with a prospect by placing a call or suggesting lunch, you can build your network of colleagues and referral partners in the same way.

You don't have to wait for word of mouth to build in order to start getting referrals. You can seek out potential referral partners by identifying people who are in contact with your target market and getting to know them. After an initial meeting or conversation, you can stay in touch using some of the same tactics as shown for direct contact and follow-up, plus these tactics more specific to networking and referral building.

### Tactics for Networking and Referral Building

- *Attending meetings and seminars.* The best way to meet people, because they have come there to meet people. Also a good follow-up technique if you keep returning to the same group.

- *Identifying referral partners*. Seek out people who serve the same clients you do, no matter what they sell. Some people get most of their business from this type of referral.

- *Exchanging materials*. An easy step to take with potential referral partners. Send them your materials and ask for theirs. Follow up further if you like.

- *Lunch or coffee (with contacts)*. A good way to get to know referral partners, colleagues, and center-of-influence types. Your goal is to get them to know, like, and trust you.

- *Office visits*. Make a date to visit your potential referral partners in their office. It makes it easy on them, and you'll get a good sense of how they operate.

- *Serving on committees*. This can be a relationship-building strategy or a visibility strategy, depending on the committee. Try for both payoffs at once.

- *Volunteering or trading services*. Volunteer your professional services for a high-profile nonprofit to get recognition. Trade services with a potential referral partner to build trust.

- *Sharing resources*. Become the person with the golden Rolodex. Share your resources with others so you can call on them when you need contacts or information.

- *Collaborating on projects*. An excellent way for a one-person business to expand contacts and visibility. Your collaborator may know another whole circle of people.

- *Swapping contacts*. Exchange leads or past clients with a referral partner in a noncompetitive business. You could even send letters introducing each other.

- *Introduction or leads groups*. A group of people who meet regularly to exchange contacts, leads, and referrals. If you can't find one you like, start your own.

- *Reading the trade press*. If you always know what's going on in your field, you will be able to take advantage of opportunities others don't even see. You can find leads there too.

 **Public Speaking**

Think of speaking in front of a group as an immensely powerful form of networking. People are much more likely to remember you if you are standing in

> "'No room at the inn! Could you recommend a barn, perhaps, with a manger?' Does that story sound familiar? As far back as biblical times, people have relied on who they know for information and referrals. That is the way we find summer camps for our children, auto mechanics, dentists, good restaurants, and countless other goods and services in our lives. The Yellow Pages are a wonderful resource, but would you use them to identify a cardiologist?
>
> "Networking for word-of-mouth advice and personal referrals is a timesaving and an 'aggravation management' technique to get recommendations for what we need. We have been exchanging those recommendations and sharing resources since Eve offered Adam an apple in the Garden of Eden. It is how the world works—and has, since the beginning of time."
>
> Susan RoAne, keynote speaker and author of *How to Work a Room* (Warner Books, 1989); *The Secrets of Savvy Networking* (Warner Books, 1993); and *What Do I Say Next?* (Warner Books, 1997)

the front of the room instead of seated in the back. If you are new to public speaking, try starting out small. Volunteer to introduce speakers at an event, or offer your services on a panel. Then gradually work your way up to solo presentations or full-length workshops.

A word of caution about public speaking: look for an already organized group to present to rather than trying to invite your own guests. (That tactic belongs under promotional events.) You may be surprised to find how many civic, business, and professional groups are eagerly seeking free speakers for their meetings.

### Tactics for Public Speaking

• *Hosting meetings.* Any excuse for standing up in front of a group will make you more visible. Serve on a program committee, or arrange to make announcements or introductions.

• *Serving on panels.* An easy way to break into public speaking without having to prepare a whole talk. Let people know you are available to speak on your area of expertise.

• *Making presentations.* Every meeting needs a speaker. Most of them are people like you, speaking for free to promote their business. It gets you visibility and credibility both.

• *Giving workshops.* If you really like to speak or teach, this is an effective way to expose prospective clients to your expertise. If they like you, they will want more of you.

 **Writing and Publicity**

Writing articles or a column about your specialty is an excellent way to gain visibility and credibility you couldn't manage on your own. If you have never been published before, association or company newsletters are often a good place to get your first exposure. Don't rule out these tactics if you're not a good writer. A ghostwriter or professional editor can help turn your words into publishable prose.

Getting interviewed by the media can be a bit harder, but you can start small here as well. Small-town newspapers like to profile local experts. If you live in a large city, try your neighborhood paper. When approaching the media, always remember that you need to provide them with a story. Tell the editor or producer exactly why readers will be interested in what you have to say. Tie-ins with holidays or with current events are often a good excuse to make contact.

A word of caution about writing and publicity: unless you are on the front page of the *New York Times*, don't expect a deluge of phone calls. You are more likely to receive congratulations from people you already know than to hear from a flock of new customers. Writing and publicity techniques are better for building your credibility and name recognition than for directly filling your marketing pipeline. An added benefit of these techniques, though, is that you will be able to include the resulting clippings or reprints in your marketing kit.

### Tactics for Writing and Publicity

• *Writing articles about your specialty.* When you publish an article, people not only read it and call you; you can send it to your mailing list for follow-up, and use it in your marketing kit.

• *Writing an advice column.* If your column appears regularly in the same publication, people who read it will remember you and think of you as an expert.

• *Being quoted by the media.* You can make this happen by sending a letter when you see your area of expertise discussed in the media. Next time, they may call you.

• *Having stories published about you.* Find a freelance writer in your field, and let her know how interesting you are. Sometimes you can even write a profile about yourself.

• *Being interviewed in print or on radio or TV.* Send a fascinating press release to editors or producers that cover your area. There's a lot of space and time to fill every day.

 **Promotional Events**

Putting on a show, or being part of someone else's, is a time-honored way of attracting customer attention. Participating in a trade show or cosponsoring a fund raiser can put you in direct contact with potential clients and bring you an audience you couldn't afford to reach alone. But look out for the cost! Buying a booth, setting up a display, and distributing literature to hundreds of people, or even more, can be extremely expensive. Try evaluating the cost per head of each solid lead you expect the event to generate, and see if you can beat that price by using some other marketing method.

If you want to try producing your own event, such as a workshop or reception, figure out how much it will cost you to bring each person to the door, and decide whether the expected business will be worth the expense. Publicizing events like this can require a substantial outlay for mailings and advertising. Look to see what the result might be if you spent the same amount of time and money on generating business through other strategies.

### Tactics for Promotional Events

• *Trade shows.* Booths at big shows can be very expensive, but many associations put on tabletop expositions. Trade shows are better for collecting leads than for closing sales.

• *"Free" demonstrations or workshops.* Offer a free demonstration or low-cost workshop to your hottest prospects. It works like public speaking, but you control the invitations.

• *Open house or reception.* Find an excuse to throw a party, and invite prospects and referral partners. People who don't return your calls will often show up here.

• *Cosponsored events.* Cosponsoring a workshop, symposium, or fund raiser with a nonprofit will attract clients who support the cause.

• *Networking lunch, breakfast, or mixer.* Invite clients, prospects, and referral partners to meet each other for their own benefit. Tell everyone to bring a guest.

 **Advertising**

Many service businesses have found advertising of any kind to be completely ineffective. Remember the know-like-and-trust factor: ads don't allow customers to get to know you personally. This doesn't mean that advertising should be completely eliminated as a possible strategy. For some service business owners, media advertising can be a reliable source of leads. For others, direct mail advertising can introduce their business to new customers. But in most cases, advertising alone rarely generates business; it must be coupled with direct contact and follow-up in order for it to pay off.

To know if you should be considering advertising, ask yourself this question: "How do customers usually select a service like mine?" If your immediate answer is "by referral," you will probably find advertising to be a waste of money. But if your customers often do make their buying decision from advertising, you may need to consider some form of it.

Take a look at your competition and see whether they are advertising. Owners of household services, such as painting or cleaning, frequently get customers from ads. If you offer a service that people need in an emergency, like plumbing or dental care, advertising may benefit you also. Professionals who market seminars or other date-dependent programs usually find direct mail to be a necessity.

Another category of service that people sometimes select through an ad is something they might be embarrassed to ask for a referral about. Debt management or psychotherapy are two examples.

Before you decide to advertise, always look at the potential return on your investment. How many customers will an ad have to bring you before it pays for itself? And is there some more effective way you could spend the money?

### Tactics for Advertising

• *Newspaper or magazine classifieds.* The more targeted your ad, the better. Ask the reader for an immediate response. Track every response you get to see if the ad is working.

• *Display ads in newspapers, magazines, and trade journals.* Ads like these are really for visibility, not direct response. You usually need a big budget, and repeat advertising, to make them work.

• *Yellow Pages.* Works well only if your service is something people will think to look for there, and your ad is one of the most noticeable. Don't waste money on a small ad in a big category.

• *Other business directories.* Follow the same rules as with the Yellow Pages, plus check into distribution before you buy. Will your potential clients actually see this directory?

• *Professional directories.* Will get you business only if people actually use it, but consider credibility also. If a certain directory is the official source for an industry, you probably want to be in it.

Margo Komenar is a business coach, marketing consultant, and the author of *Electronic Marketing* (Wiley, 1997). She recommends five key strategies for those who market their own services:

1. *Establish yourself as an expert in your field or as a specialist within your area of expertise.* Write articles, give seminars, and teach courses. Find web sites with the same audience as your target market, and contribute content, or host on-line chats.

2. *Demonstrate your services.* Give people a sample in a free newsletter, low-cost workshop, or complimentary consultation.

3. *Leverage your client and colleague relationships.* Form partnerships with other people in business whose products and services are related to your own. Promote your services jointly, or exchange introductions to each other's clients.

4. *Serve before selling; offer something of value.* Send information to your prospects that you know they will find useful, and let them find out about your services by getting to know you, rather than by giving them a sales pitch.

5. *Become an information resource, respected and sought out as an industry spokesperson.* Build a web site that is a community resource rather than a brochure. Publish a print, e-mail, or fax newsletter, and distribute it through companies and organizations that reach your target market. Offer to interview potential clients for your publication, and use this opportunity to build rapport.

Margo Komenar, M.A., business coach and
marketing consultant, www.komenar.com

• *Event or conference programs.* Another visibility booster that may need a big budget. Works best if people who already know you will notice the ad.

• *Direct mail.* Has nowhere near the impact of a personal letter. For consulting and professional services, it's often a waste of money. Narrow your target, and use direct contact instead. For personal or household services, evaluate the cost of your potential return.

• *Flyer distribution.* Flyers are cheaper than throwing brochures around, and can be used to develop interest with a targeted group. They work best if a limited time offer is included.

- *Radio or TV ads*. You need a substantial budget to go this route. Ads must be repeated to have any effect. If you do this, get professional help in scripting your ad.

- *Web site*. A web site alone is just a tool, not a complete strategy. You must let people know your site is there to have an impact. Think of it as a very sophisticated brochure.

- *Billboards*. For personal or professional services? Well, people have done it. You can probably find better ways to spend the money…like any of the other tactics already mentioned.

After reading this overview of potential marketing strategies and tactics, you should have some preliminary idea of which strategies you might like to use in your Get Clients Now! program. Consider which two, three, or four strategies you think you would most like to employ. More than four strategies are too many to attempt in a 28-day period, and fewer than two won't give you enough flexibility.

## But What About Selling?

In thinking about what marketing strategies to use, it may have occurred to you to ask where selling enters the picture. This is another way in which marketing a service business differs from marketing a product. When you are selling a service, marketing and sales are not two separate activities that occur at different times; instead, they must be seamlessly integrated. Think about it. If you are talking to someone about what you do, you may think you are networking. But if she expresses an interest in doing business with you, you are instantly in a selling situation.

The exact opposite is equally true: if you make contact with a prospect in order to sell your service, the person may tell you that he isn't interested but has a colleague who might be. Then you would switch from selling to networking.

The marketing strategy of direct contact and follow-up could also be thought of as personal selling. But it would be misleading to call it that, since in many cases when you make contact, you are not "selling" at all. You may be asking a potential customer how her business is going or what her needs are. You could be inviting her to your upcoming open house or speaking engagement. The fact is, when you are personally telling a prospect what you do, selling can happen at any point.

So think about everything you do to get clients as being both marketing and sales at the same time. Consider every marketing strategy as a selling strategy, and vice versa.

Tony Alessandra, the author of 13 books, including *Collaborative Selling* (Wiley, 1993) and *Charisma* (Warner Books, 1998), points to experienced salespeople as a powerful model for people selling their own services.

"The successful sales rep seems to just sit back and respond to calls. The orders roll in, and she seems to be getting rich without effort. What we generally don't see are the years she spent building her network and investing in her personal visibility.

"This successful salesperson is using personal marketing. She's marketing herself just as a company would market a product. Just as it takes time to build brand loyalty, it takes time and hard work for personal marketing to pay off, but it's worth it in the long run. If your best potential customers have been made aware of you in advance of your contact with them, you'll find it much easier to set up an appointment, establish a relationship, and consummate the sale.

"Keep in mind that it's better to work on getting multiple exposures to a smaller target group than to spread your effort and have fewer exposures to more people. Potential customers in your target market should be reading your articles, receiving mail from you, hearing you speak or give a seminar, bumping into you at a social function or trade show, and hearing about you and your expertise from their fellow association members and friends.

"The reason it's so important to invest your time in these methods is that the quality of an incoming lead is almost always better than the lead you get in a cold call. The prospect who calls you has already identified his need for your service, and he's calling to get your help.

"When you effectively use personal marketing, you'll find that little by little, people will start to recognize your name, your company, your product, and your face. Pretty soon the phone will start to ring for you, and your image as an established expert will start to take hold."

Tony Alessandra, Ph.D., speaker and author,
www.alessandra.com

## A Word About Terminology

Before moving on to the next chapter, it might be helpful to review some of the terminology. Up to this point, you have encountered marketing strategies, tac-

Laura Whitworth was one of the first professional and personal coaches in the United States. Now a director of the Coaches Training Institute, Laura remembers what she learned when she was first building her coaching practice: "My secrets for getting clients can be boiled down to what I call the Five P's of Enrollment:

"1. *Passion*. You have to have passion for your product, be clear that it works, and know that the service you offer is a gift to people.

"2. *Push*. When you need to push something big, like a refrigerator, you first have to give it a real strong surge, and then you just keep on. It's that strong surge that gets you past being uncomfortable about promoting yourself. If it's tied to your passion, the push can come automatically. The big push at the beginning really helped me.

"3. *Persistence*. After that first big push, you need to keep on pushing. Persistence keeps you going over and over again, sometimes with no evidence that what you are doing is working, or in the face of dwindling resources.

"4. *Patience*. This was what really worked for me—trusting that as time went by, I would get better at marketing myself. I was out there pushing in the world when there was no understanding of what coaching was. I had to persist and be patient, and it continued to grow. If you planted a garden, and expected the harvest the day after you planted the seeds, or the month after, you would be a pretty naive gardener. Most people want immediate results, but you need a long-term view. Now I'm a leader in the field and I don't do anything to fill my practice.

"5. *Profit*. That's the result of it all, and in more than the financial sense. Your clients profit by working with you, and you profit personally by doing what you are passionate about."

Laura Whitworth, Certified Professional and Personal Coach, Coaches Training Institute, www.TheCoaches.com

tics, and types of impact. Each overall strategy (e.g., direct contact and follow-up) is made up of tactics (e.g., cold calling, warm calling, and canvassing), and has a resulting impact (outreach, visibility, or credibility). In a few pages, you will also learn about stages of the marketing cycle. If you remember the distinctions among these terms and the elements they represent, you will be able to follow the process of building your Get Clients Now! program more easily.

# Chapter 2

# Where Do You Start?
# The Marketing and Sales Cycle

*You can't just sit there and wait for people to give you that golden dream; you've got to get out there and make it happen for yourself.*

—Diana Ross

## The Universal Marketing Cycle

Marketing and sales operates on a predictable cycle, with four separate stages:

1. Filling the pipeline
2. Following up
3. Getting presentations
4. Closing sales

The activities that take place within each stage of the cycle will vary depending on your business, but the cycle is the same for everyone. Knowing more about how this cycle works will enable you to determine exactly where to focus more time and energy in your marketing.

Figure 2-1 shows the marketing cycle as a water system. At the top are the collection buckets for the prospects, contacts, leads, and referrals with which you are filling the pipeline. In your office or briefcase, these will be represented by the names and phone numbers of people and organizations. *Prospects* are people you attract using a visibility strategy, such as publicity or advertising. *Contacts* are people you meet through outreach strategies like networking, or just in the course of business or life. *Leads* are people you identify through research or hear about from your contacts. And *referrals* are people who are referred to you by contacts, clients, and others.

Don't worry too much about the distinctions among these categories. They are all people in your pipeline.

**Figure 2-1. The universal marketing cycle.**

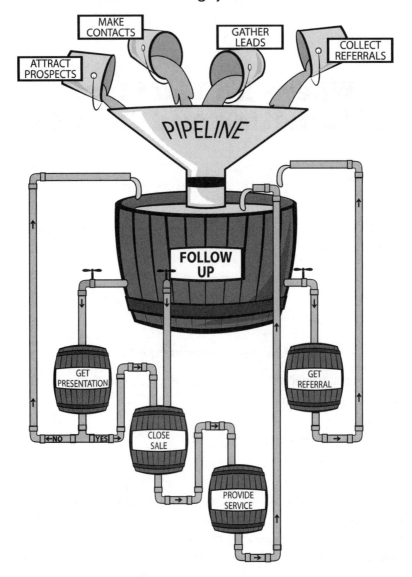

The marketing pipeline empties into the follow-up pool, which you dip into in order to move potential clients and referral sources further along in the system. Your goal is to keep the follow-up pool constantly circulating, with new prospects entering the pipeline and existing ones flowing into the next stage of the cycle.

The arrows in the bottom half of the diagram indicate the direction of flow. With potential clients, you want to move quickly to getting the presentation. This is where you find out about their needs, tell them more about what you do, and see if there is a match between the two of you. The actual presentation

"Get Clients Now! is the program I chose to offer through the North Hollywood/Universal City Chamber of Commerce, and last year a colleague agreed to participate in order to fill a group about to begin. That's the seminar leader's equivalent of a doctor's professional courtesy. But he slammed right up against his own pattern of excuses when he realized that he was constantly filling the pipeline through networking and had in fact, become a networking junkie.

"He decided to create a system of checks and balances that made him follow up with the people he meets at one function before he attends another. Now he fills his own programs with paying clients instead of colleagues who attend out of professional courtesy."

Cat Williford, Certified Professional and Personal Coach

may happen formally or informally, in person, by telephone, or even by mail. When the presentation concludes, you may be ready to ask for the business, or you may need to prepare a detailed proposal first. In some cases, the presentation stage may last 15 minutes, and in others, it can take many months.

Your desired result, though, is always the same: to move prospects forward to closing the sale. If they say yes at the end of the presentation, you have done it. If they say no, back they go into the follow-up pool, where you continue to follow up with them as long as it seems worthwhile. Sometimes follow-up will lead directly to closing the sale after all, and at other times, you may need to make yet another presentation.

When the sale is closed, you begin to provide service. As you are providing service, and after you complete providing service, the client must also stay in the follow-up pool. By continuing to follow up with this client, you may close another sale or get referrals.

Some of the people and organizations in your pipeline may never enter the prospect area of the cycle at all. They may be contacts who can be referral sources for you. You must follow up with these people also, regularly reminding them that you are around, thanking them for referrals, and putting them right back in the follow-up pool.

In any of these cases, what follow-up looks like and how often it happens depends on the nature of your business and the type of contact that seems natural for you. Refer to the tactics listed in the previous chapter under direct contact and follow-up. Every one of these is a potential follow-up technique.

## How Does the Cycle Work?

Let's look at two examples. Suppose you are a computer systems consultant who typically works with large corporate clients. At a breakfast meeting of the Association of Management Systems Professionals, you met the director of management information systems (MIS) of a major corporation. You spoke for a few moments about his company and exchanged business cards. The director is now a contact in your marketing pipeline.

When you returned to your office, you entered his name and other information into the contact management system on your computer and put him on the system's calendar for a follow-up call the next day. He is now in your follow-up pool.

The next day, the MIS director's name and phone number popped up on the automatic tickler list displayed on your computer. You called him, got his voice mail, and left a message reminding him of your meeting, briefly describing the kind of work you do, and suggesting it might be to his benefit if the two of you were to talk. Then you put him on the calendar for another follow-up three days later.

The MIS director did not return your call, so when he popped up on your tickler list again in three days, you placed another call. This time you reached him, but he didn't have time to talk. He did mention, however, that some changes were coming in his company that might indicate a need for your services. With this new information, the MIS director is now a prospect rather than just a contact. He is still in the follow-up pool.

You now send the MIS director a letter, telling him how you could be helpful to him during this upcoming project. You enclose some biographical information about you, a summary of the type of services you provide, and a list of satisfied clients. A week after sending the letter, you call him again. After three phone calls over ten days, you once again reach him in person. This time you suggest a meeting, and he agrees to meet next week. He has just moved from the follow-up pool to the presentation stage.

At the presentation, you spend about half the time asking questions and learning about his company and the upcoming project. Then you describe how you can help him and why you are uniquely qualified to do so. You answer his questions about your background and expertise. At the end of an hour, you ask if he is interested in using you on this project. He asks you to prepare a proposal, outlining what you would do and how much it would cost. You agree, and before leaving you schedule a time with him a week later to go over the proposal in person. At this point, the MIS director is still in the presentation stage.

One week later, you meet with him to discuss your completed proposal. You explain what you have written and the rationale for your process and pricing. After answering his questions about the proposal, you ask if he is ready to sign a contract with you. He tells you he must discuss your proposal with the CEO before making a decision. You make sure he has all the information he needs for that discussion, and offer to be present at the meeting. He declines your offer but tells you he will decide within two weeks. The MIS director has now moved from the presentation stage back into the follow-up pool.

Two weeks pass without the MIS director's calling you, so you call him. After several days of telephone tag, he tells you that the CEO has not yet had time to meet with him and suggests you try back in another couple of weeks. You do call back after two more weeks go by, and, wonder of wonders, the MIS director says the CEO is in favor of hiring you. You ask him when you can get to work, and he suggests you come to a project planning meeting next Monday. Congratulations! You have just closed the sale.

That the entire process took over two months from beginning to end is not unusual. Much longer cycles than this are common, whether your clients are big companies or single individuals. Follow-up is in the center of the universal marketing cycle diagram for a reason: consistent and persistent follow-up is central to moving a prospect forward to making a sale.

Now for our second example, let's say you are a career counselor whose clients are professionals in job transition. You gave a talk entitled "Managing Your Career" to the Professional Women's Network. At the end of your presentation, you asked for anyone who was interested in working with you personally to give you a business card. Three women in the audience—Elsa, Mindy, and Dolores—gave you cards. They are now prospects in your marketing pipeline.

The following morning, you stapled each card to a page in your prospects notebook and noted where and when you met these women. You sent each a copy of your brochure with a personal note. In your daily planner, you entered an action item for one week later to place follow-up calls to all three. They are now in your follow-up pool. Two days later, Elsa called you. She had read your brochure and wanted to find out how much you charge. The moment you picked up the phone, Elsa was in the presentation stage.

You asked Elsa to tell you about her situation and explained how you thought you could help. After making sure she understood what she was getting for her money, you told her your rates and asked if she wanted to make an appointment. She said yes. You have just closed the sale with Elsa. And, of course, five days later, you will still call Mindy and Dolores, who remain in your follow-up pool.

## Choosing Where to Focus

The universal marketing cycle is a clever diagnostic tool to help you choose where to focus your marketing efforts. Think about your own situation as you review the cycle. Where in the system are you stuck? What stage of your marketing needs the most work:

1. *Filling the pipeline*—having enough phone numbers to call?

2. *Following up*—calling the phone numbers you already have?

3. *Getting presentations*—getting from follow-up to presentation?

4. *Closing sales*—getting from presentation to sale?

In most businesses, telephoning your contacts is one of the primary methods of follow-up, so having enough phone numbers to call is an easy test to see if your pipeline is sufficiently full. But if you are in a business where directly soliciting clients is inappropriate, such as psychotherapy or, in some cases, law, ask yourself if enough people are calling you. Another good test is to imagine you were using a newsletter for follow-up. How many people who already know you could you send it to?

Do you already know where you are stuck? If so, skip ahead to the next section. If not, try asking yourself some questions.

If you answer yes to the following questions, you need to focus on *filling the pipeline:*

- Are you brand-new in business?

- If you sat down to call every lead you currently have, would you be through before lunch?

- Have you already called every prospect in your book within the past 30 days?

- Are you not calling the prospects you have because you already know they don't need you or can't afford you?

- Are you in a business where it's either unethical or inappropriate to call on prospective clients, and your phone just isn't ringing?

If you answer yes to the following questions, you need to concentrate on *following up:*

- Do you have a drawer full of business cards from people you have met but have not spoken to since then?

- Have colleagues handed you leads whom you haven't gotten around to calling?

Where Do You Start? The Marketing and Sales Cycle | 29 |

- Are there prospects who said no or didn't return your initial call whom you haven't contacted in the past three months?

- Do you have a wide network of personal contacts with whom you never talk business?

- Are there people you haven't been in touch with who inquired about your services in the past, but weren't quite ready or didn't have the funds?

If you answer yes to the following questions, you should work on *getting presentations:*

- Do you follow up with prospective clients consistently, but can't seem to get an initial meeting?

- Do people refuse to take your call, or brush you off quickly when you do get through to them?

- Are all your prospects already working with a competitor— or at least that's what they say?

- Does everyone you talk to seem to think what you do is too expensive, will take too much time, or is just not for them?

Finally, if you answer yes to the following questions, it's time to concentrate on *closing sales:*

- Are you regularly getting to the presentation stage, but don't seem to close enough sales?

- Do your prospects seem to be going through the motions of allowing you to present, but have no serious interest?

- Are you encountering objection after objection that prevents the sale from going through?

- Do you often walk out of a presentation not knowing where the client stands?

## What Needs the Most Work?

Once you know where you are stuck, it's time to choose where you will focus your marketing efforts for the next 28 days. If you think you need work in more than one stage of the universal marketing cycle, start with the first one in the sequence. For example, if you feel stuck on both follow-up and getting presentations, choose follow-up. If you aren't sure where to start, begin with filling the pipeline. And if that's not really where the problem is, you will find out soon enough, and move forward to the right stage anyway. Just be sure to pick only one.

> "When helping my clients with their marketing, we'll often be working on how to contact new prospects most effectively. We'll look at associations, directories, and mailing lists, and discuss the most appropriate ways to get prospects' attention and get in front of them. Then I ask whom they know in their current network of business associates and past clients to contact as well.
>
> "It's not unusual that they have a contact list of several dozen, if not several hundred, people whom they have some business connection with. When I hear this, I suggest they put any cold contacts on a back burner for now, and pay closer attention on how to pick all that 'low-hanging fruit.'
>
> "The truth is, you may not need to make as much effort as you thought to generate new clients. They may be closer than you think. Still, you need a plan to contact these people and make the best of those contacts."
>
> Robert Middleton, marketing consultant, Action Plan
> Marketing, www.actionplan.com

Now that you have chosen which stage of the universal marketing cycle to focus on, the first step toward designing your own personal Get Clients Now! program is to determine which marketing strategies you should use. Look at the following list to find out what impact your marketing needs to have in each stage of the universal marketing cycle.

### What Impact Do You Need?

| If you chose... | The impact you need is... |
|---|---|
| Filling the pipeline | 1. Outreach |
| | 2. Visibility |
| Following up | 1. Outreach |
| Getting presentations | 1. Outreach |
| | 2. Visibility |
| | 3. Credibility |
| Closing sales | 1. Outreach |
| | 2. Credibility |
| | 3. Visibility |

Where more than one impact is listed, they are in priority order. So if you are stuck on getting presentations, for example, you should generally concentrate the most effort on outreach strategies, less effort on visibility strategies and the least amount on credibility strategies. For filling the pipeline, notice that credibility is not particularly important, so it doesn't have to be a factor in choosing marketing strategies. And for follow-up, the only impact you should be concerned with is outreach, so forget about visibility and credibility strategies for now.

Here is a summary of the strategies, listed by impact, so you can revisit the choices you made in Chapter 1.

### What Strategies Should You Use?

| If you need the impact of... | You should use the strategies... |
| --- | --- |
| Outreach | 1. Direct contact and follow-up |
| | 2. Networking and referral building |
| Visibility | 1. Networking and referral building |
| | 2. Public speaking |
| | 3. Writing and publicity |
| | 4. Promotional events |
| | 5. Advertising |
| Credibility | 1. Public speaking |
| | 2. Writing and publicity |

"A good marketing plan is based on knowing everything there is to know about your business and the grass-roots community it is nestled in," maintains Claude Whitmyer. "It's having a well-thought-out calendar of marketing activities, using marketing vehicles that are appropriate to the circle of intimacy that you are targeting." In his book *Running a One-Person Business* (Ten Speed Press, 1994), written with coauthor Salli Rasberry, Claude presents what he calls the Five Laws of Grassroots Marketing:

1. The best time to market is when you don't need more business.

2. The best source of new clients is old clients.

3. Market for quality, not quantity.

4. Your best marketing vehicle is a satisfied client.

5. Customer retention is the measure of successful marketing.

Claude Whitmyer, author, Center for Good Work,
www.futureu.com/goodbiz.html

For each impact, the strategies are listed in order of effectiveness. It's a good idea to employ the most effective strategies, unless there is some reason that a particular strategy won't work for you. If you are afraid of speaking in public, for example, you might choose writing articles to build your credibility instead.

What are the best strategies for your situation? Review the two, three, or four marketing strategies you tentatively picked in Chapter 1 against the appropriate strategies for the stage of the universal marketing cycle you are working on. Choosing specific marketing strategies to use consistently is one of the most important ways the program will help you to focus your efforts. Therefore, you will need to stick with the strategies you choose now for the entire program.

## The Get Clients Now! Action Worksheet

You are ready to begin working with the action worksheet (Figure 2-2), the central planning tool for your own Get Clients Now! 28-day program. (Because you may wish to use the Get Clients Now! system over and over again, make an enlarged photocopy of the blank worksheet in Figure 2-2 to serve as the form you will fill out.)

The action worksheet is where you will first record the six key components of your program. When you have completed the planning phase of your program in Chapter 5, you will be transferring some of these components to the tracking worksheet described in Chapter 6.

### The Key Components of the Get Clients Now! Program

1. *Marketing strategies*—the two to four strategies you will be using during the month of the program.

2. *Marketing stage*—the stage of the universal marketing cycle where you are stuck or which you need to work on more.

3. *Program goal*—the goal of your program, that is, the results you plan to achieve in the next 28 days. You will set the goal in Chapter 3.

4. *Success ingredients*—the missing ingredients you need to be successful in your marketing, and that you plan to create during the program. You will discover these in Chapter 4.

5. *Daily actions*—ten specific steps you plan to take on a daily or weekly basis over the next 28 days. You will choose these in Chapter 5.

**Figure 2-2. Action worksheet.**

# *GET CLIENTS NOW!*™ Action Worksheet

What strategies will you use?

|  |  |  |  |  |  |
|---|---|---|---|---|---|
| 1. DIRECT CONTACT AND FOLLOW-UP | 2. NETWORKING AND REFERRAL BUILDING | 3. PUBLIC SPEAKING | 4. WRITING AND PUBLICITY | 5. PROMOTIONAL EVENTS | 6. ADVERTISING |
| ☐ | ☐ | ☐ | ☐ | ☐ | ☐ |

Where are you stuck?   ☐ Filling the pipeline   ☐ Following up   ☐ Getting presentations   ☐ Closing sales

How much business do you have now? _____

How much business do you *really* want? _____

What would that get you? _____

_____

What is your program goal? _____

What will be your reward? _____

Success Ingredients                                                                 Target Date

1. _____   _____

2. _____   _____

3. _____   _____

Daily Actions

1. _____

2. _____

3. _____

4. _____

5. _____

6. _____

7. _____

8. _____

9. _____

10. _____

Special Permission _____

6. *Special permission*—the permission you need to grant your-self to be successful in areas where you may have failed in the past. There is more about this in Chapter 5 also.

Make your first entries on the worksheet now. Check the boxes that corre-spond to the marketing strategies you will be using, and the stage of the uni-versal marketing cycle where you are stuck: filling the pipeline, following up, getting presentations, or closing sales. Now let's go on to the next step: setting a sales and marketing goal.

---

Nido Qubein is chairman of an international consulting firm; board member of numerous universities, companies, and non-profit organizations; an award-winning speaker; and the author of dozens of business books, including *Stairway to Success* (Wiley, 1997). Now a multimillionaire, Nido came to this country as a teenager, "without connections, no money, and no knowledge of the English language." Nido believes there are four principles of success for anyone in business:

1. Have a clear vision of your business.

2. Have a solid strategy for making necessary changes and achieving your goals.

3. Have practical systems to help you achieve your goal.

4. The best ideas, principles, or talents are useless unless they are executed consistently.

"I learned English by memorizing ten new words a day," Nido remembers. "Each day, I would review the words I had learned the day before and then study 10 new ones. By the end of the week, I had added 70 new words to my vocabulary. It was this consistent effort that enabled me to achieve fluency in English."

Nido R. Qubein,
Chairman, Creative Services

# Chapter 3

# Where Are You Headed?
# Setting Your Sales and
# Marketing Goal

*We can achieve what we can conceive and believe.*

—Mark Twain

### The Seven Keys to Achievement

In this chapter, you are going to set your sales and marketing goal for the 28 days of the Get Clients Now! program. Let's begin by putting this process into perspective. There are seven keys to achievement of any goal or project, and they are the basis of the system:

1. *Focus.* You will be looking at your program goal, success ingredient projects, and list of daily actions each morning, which will keep them in the forefront of your mind. Knowing that you have only 28 days to achieve the results you want will tighten your focus on marketing and help you to ignore distractions.

2. *Evidence.* The program will give you a constant reality check on how you are doing. It will tell you right away if you are not working hard enough or are spending precious marketing time on activities like cleaning out your file drawer. It will also tell you when you have done enough and can take a day off without guilt. By constantly measuring your level of effort and comparing it to the results you create, you will learn to make much smarter decisions about what to do (and not do) in marketing.

3. *Direction.* For the next 28 days, you don't need to worry about what to do to get more clients. Your tracking worksheet will tell you. Just complete your daily actions first each day; then spend whatever marketing time you have left on your success ingredients.

4. *Motivation*. Allow the program to act as a motivational device. Put your tracking worksheet up on the wall where you will see it often. Run a contest with yourself to see how early in the day you can complete your daily actions, and then try to beat your own record. Set up a reward for finishing each success ingredient project or reaching a certain percentage mark toward your program goal. Invent your own "getting clients" game, using the tracking worksheet as your scorecard. Make up your own rules; the more fun you can have, the easier the next 28 days will be.

These four keys to achievement will begin to work for you automatically as soon as you begin the program. With just these four factors in place, you will substantially increase your likelihood of success in marketing. To stack the odds even more in your favor, look for help from the remaining three achievement keys:

5. *Accountability*. Have someone other than yourself to whom you are accountable—who will ask you once or twice a week what you have done so far, and what's next.

6. *Perspective*. Get a different point of view on your progress or your challenges. Just hearing your problem restated by another person can give you insight that will help you find a solution. When you are feeling low because you haven't reached your goal yet, it's also great to have someone point out that you are more than halfway there.

7. *Support*. It's helpful to have someone else to complain to or celebrate out loud with—someone who cares about your progress. If you are up against a roadblock, grousing about it for a few minutes may be all you need to get back into action. And having someone to share your success with can make it much sweeter.

You could use your spouse, best friend, or business partner to provide these extra three keys, but the individuals closest to you may not be the best choice. The people in your personal life will not always be thrilled that you plan to spend more time on marketing, and your business associates may tend to sidetrack you with immediate problems or day-to-day management tasks. You may find it more helpful to look for accountability, perspective, and support from someone with more detachment yet who clearly understands the importance you are placing this month on achieving your marketing goals. The best way to get this extra advantage is from a business buddy, action group, or personal coach.

A *business buddy* is a friend or colleague who also wants help to get into action and stay on track. The two of you assist each other in reaching your goals by setting up a regular check-in, with each of you reporting on progress, announcing successes, and stating challenges. The buddy's job is to listen, celebrate, commiserate, and be a brainstorming partner.

*Action groups* serve the same function for a group of people who wish to work together. You may be able to find an existing group with a business or marketing focus (sometimes called success teams, goals groups, or resource groups) through local periodicals or business organizations. If you would like to be part of a group whose members are all using the Get Clients Now! program, you can find a list of such groups on the web site: www.GetClientsNow.com. Some groups have a professional leader, while others have each member take turns leading.

You can also hire your own *personal coach*—a professional who is trained in assisting people to set and achieve goals. Either ask your friends and colleagues whether they have worked with a coach they could refer you to, or get a list of coaches who are familiar with this program from the Get Clients Now! web site.

Keep in mind that support from a buddy, group, or coach does not have to involve in-person meetings and travel time. Many groups meet via teleconference or on-line chat, and your buddy or coach can work with you by phone or e-mail.

Whether you are going it alone or getting some outside help in sticking to the program, remember the seven keys to achievement over the next 28 days. Keep your goal, projects, and action plan constantly visible, and allow some of their magic to work for you.

## What Is a Goal, Anyway?

A *goal* is a statement of intention. It is your own personal declaration of what you want, what you plan to focus on, and what you intend to accomplish.

> "In the early phases of a dream, or with a big dream, there may be no evidence that your idea is a good one, or that this is the right time to execute it. At that moment, it is essential that you believe in yourself and in your dream. Your belief will be the foundation, a place that you can stand on and say, 'I'm going for it because it matters to me, and I believe in my dreams.' Then prove you really do believe in yourself by taking action.
>
> "Make the call, write the letter, map out an action plan, hire a coach, share your dream. Do something, and do it now!"
>
> Marcia Wieder, speaker and author of *Making Your Dreams Come True* (Master Media, 1993) and *Doing Less and Having More* (Morrow, 1998), www.marciaw.com

Having a sales and marketing goal gives you a destination in your business journey. Only when you know where you are going can you choose the right-path to get you there. And you have to be clear about your destination to know when you have arrived.

Many years ago, some unsung hero (or heroine) of goal-setting came up with the acronym SMART to describe the five important characteristics of a meaningful goal:

Specific          It spells out the target you are aiming for very precisely.

Measurable    It states the target in such a way that you can measure exactly when you have arrived, as well as how far along you are at any specific moment.

Achievable     It is physically possible to accomplish within whatever limits you must consider.

Realistic        It can be accomplished within the specified time and with the resources you have available.

Timed            There is a calendar date by which you plan to achieve it.

Here are some examples of SMART goals:

Two new clients with signed contracts by the end of the program

Fifteen paying appointments scheduled weekly beginning in Week 2

Twenty-two billable hours worked per week for the full month

Five thousand dollars in business booked for the following month by Week 3

Six new qualified prospects by the end of the program

The function of a goal is, first of all, to get you into action. If you have a specific target that must be accomplished by a particular date, you will perform tasks that would otherwise languish on a to-do list. A goal also keeps you on track. At any moment, you can ask yourself, "Will this [action, decision, etc.] move me closer to my goal?" Finally, having a goal gives you a way to measure your effectiveness. If you are moving toward your goal, your actions are effective; if you are not moving toward it, they are ineffective, or not effective enough.

Now you're ready to set a goal. As you answer the questions in the next section, write your responses on your action worksheet. See the sample worksheet in Figure 3-1 for an example.

## Setting a Goal for the Program

The place to start in setting a goal is to look at where you are starting from. How much business do you have now? Answer this question in whatever

**Figure 3-1. Beginning to fill out the action worksheet.**

## GET CLIENTS NOW!™ Action Worksheet

What strategies will you use?

| 1. DIRECT CONTACT AND FOLLOW-UP | 2. NETWORKING AND REFERRAL BUILDING | 3. PUBLIC SPEAKING | 4. WRITING AND PUBLICITY | 5. PROMOTIONAL EVENTS | 6. ADVERTISING |
| --- | --- | --- | --- | --- | --- |
| ☑ | ☑ | ☐ | ☐ | ☐ | ☐ |

Where are you stuck?  ☑ Filling the pipeline   ☐ Following up   ☐ Getting presentations   ☐ Closing sales

How much business do you have now? _11 clients_

How much business do you *really* want? _20 clients_

What would that get you? _pay off my credit cards, take a vacation, feel less stressed_

What is your program goal? _4 new clients by the end of the program_

What will be your reward? _go on a ski weekend_

Success Ingredients                                                                                                 Target Date

1. _____   _____

2. _____   _____

3. _____   _____

Daily Actions

1. _____

2. _____

3. _____

4. _____

5. _____

6. _____

7. _____

8. _____

9. _____

10. _____

Special Permission _____

numerical terms you typically use to measure the amount of business you currently have—for example, (1) the number of clients you have, (2) the quantity of paying appointments weekly or monthly, (3) the billable hours you have put in or expect, or (4) the dollar amount of business you have booked or already billed.

If you do not already have a way to measure business that works for you, consider what would inform your marketing efforts the most. What number would best tell you whether your marketing is succeeding? Following are some examples:

| If you are a(n)... | Your measurement might be... |
|---|---|
| Account representative | Total number of accounts |
| Personal coach | Total number of retainer clients |
| Realtor | Total number of listings |
| Contract trainer | Monthly number of training days scheduled |
| Image consultant | Monthly number of appointments booked |
| Psychotherapist | Weekly number of sessions held |
| Attorney | Billable hours worked monthly |
| Graphic designer | Billable hours worked weekly |
| Management consultant | Billable days scheduled monthly |
| Freelance writer | Dollar amount of assignments booked monthly |
| Interior designer | Dollar amount invoiced monthly |
| Salesperson | Dollar volume of sales closed monthly |

The important thing to notice about all of these measurements is that they are based on numbers you can easily keep updated and track. During the Get Clients Now! program, you will be measuring progress toward your goal each day, so you always must be able to know exactly where you are. If you are a salesperson, for example, it will be probably be easier for you to track the dollar volume of your closed sales than the amount of commission that will be calculated for you at month-end. Be sure to pick a measurement that you can know on a daily basis.

Now, using the measure you chose, ask yourself how much business you really want: not just what you want by the end of the month, but the pie-in-the-sky, wave-your-magic-wand answer. Don't worry too much about how possible it seems. Allow yourself to think big. Whatever answer you give here is the *direction* you are headed in.

If you had what you really want—that level of business you just named—what would that get you? Would it give you something tangible you have always desired, like enough money to take a European vacation? Or is an intangible outcome more important to you, such as peace of mind or a feeling of success? There's no one correct response here, so choose something that is personally exciting, inspiring, or fulfilling. This answer is your *motivation*.

Still using the same measure, what is your program goal for the month of the Get Clients Now! program? Four new clients? Fifteen paying appointments per week? Twenty-two billable hours booked weekly? A monthly gross of $5,000? Your goal is what will give you the *evidence* that your program is working (or not).

Remember the SMART goal-setting characteristics in designing your monthly goal. A program goal must be a measurable target. "More clients" is not a goal; it is a wish. In order for a goal to help you track your progress, it must be numeric because you will be measuring your progress numerically as you move through the program. Your goal should also be a bit of a stretch. Be realistic, but challenge yourself to choose something slightly ambitious.

Finally, if you achieve your goal for the month, what will be your reward? Will you buy yourself a present, take some extra time off, have a special dinner? Choose something that will really represent success to you and that you will look forward to having earned at the program's end.

By answering the questions above, you have immediately put in motion three of the seven keys to achievement: *direction, motivation,* and *evidence*. By taking this simple step, you are already on the path to success. It's part of the magic of goal setting. When you set a specific goal and begin checking your progress against it on a regular basis, your day-to-day activities start to shift in the direction that supports your goal. This happens without any conscious effort on your part. And, of course, additional effort in an informed direction can dramatically enhance the process, as you will find out in Chapter 4.

## Time for a Reality Check

Setting a realistic goal is important to your success. Choosing a target that is too easy to hit won't stretch you. You need to make an extra effort to produce your best results. But if you set a goal that is unreasonably high, you will become frustrated and discouraged. So how do you know if your goal is realistic? Here are four different ways of checking the reality of your goal. Choose whichever one you like best, or use all four:

> "When your intention is clear, when you're in touch with what it's really all about for you, it opens the floodgates. It's like the universe is waiting to give you what you want. Synchronicity occurs; serendipitous events happen. Clear intention keeps you centered in the face of all the pain, fear, and self-doubt that we experience on our way to success."
>
> Shannon Seek, Certified Professional and Personal Coach, Seek Solutions, www.SeekSolutions.com

1. *Straight-face test.* One way to use this method is to state your goal out loud, to an audience, in a strong, confident voice. If you can keep a straight face, it's probably realistic. Another way is to ask yourself the question, "Can I *really* do this?" If the most honest answer you can give yourself is a resounding "Yes!" it is most likely a realistic goal.

2. *Prior experience.* If the straight-face method seems too simplistic, review your prior experience. Have you ever had a month where you reached the level of success implied by your current goal? If you have, no matter how improbable the set of circumstances was the last time, your goal is still realistic. If you did it before, you can do it again. And remembering that your goal is supposed to be a bit of a stretch, if you even came close to your current goal in some prior month, consider it realistic.

3. *Numerical analysis.* If you got an inconclusive answer using the first method or are lacking sufficient experience to use the second, try looking at the numbers. Let's say you want to get four new clients this month. How many people do you think you will have to make presentations to in order to get four clients? Eight? Twelve? How many people will you need to speak with to set up that many presentations? Forty? One hundred twenty? Don't worry if you don't know for sure; just take a guess.

However many you think it is, do you have that many people already in your pipeline, and enough time to speak with them all? Sit down with your calculator, and crunch some numbers. Starting from where you are right now, with the resources you have available, can you deliver the level of effort needed to reach your stated goal in one month?

"A participant in one of my groups told me that what she got from the Get Clients Now! program that I use was much more valuable than reaching the goal she had set. She learned to be more compassionate with herself. What she discovered was that she had always set unrealistic goals—too high or too big—which in turn consistently set her up to fail.

"She realized that what she really needed to do was set smaller, more realistic goals. Then she experienced the feeling of winning, which greatly reduced the stress she used to suffer from. By focusing on these smaller steps, she found that she had more energy, and her mental focus was clearer than it had been in a long time."

Ricki Rush, Certified Professional
and Personal Coach, LifeWorks!,
www.lifeworks-coaching.com

Brian Azar, who calls himself "The Sales Doctor," coaches entrepreneurs and salespeople. He believes that failure to set goals is one of the primary reasons that people are unsuccessful in business. Without a goal, Brian says, all you have is a "dream or vague desire that you hope will someday come true." So if goals are this important, why do so many of us avoid them? Here is Brian's answer as to why people do not set goals:

1. *They aren't serious.* It's just words, not action. They need to reverse that—to action, not just words.

2. *They aren't accepting responsibility for their lives.* They are waiting for their ship to come in—a winning lottery ticket, a lucky break. But who else will take responsibility for your life, if not you?

3. *They were raised in a negative atmosphere.* The household attitude was, "You can't do that" or "Who do you think you are?" and they still think that way.

4. *They are afraid of criticism, of being ridiculed when trying to rise above the norm.* This makes them fear to share their goals with others, which helps to doom their success. They need to associate with people who understand the importance of goal setting and will help them reach their goals.

5. *They are afraid of failure.* This greatest deterrent keeps people in their "comfort zone." In that place they are already successful, so there is little chance for failure. But the wise individual understands that failure isn't failure at all. It is a lesson, a temporary glitch on the way to accomplishing the goal.

Brian Azar, coach, author, and speaker,
The Sales Catalyst, Inc., www.salesdoctor.com

4. *Peer comparison.* Have others you would consider peers accomplished a similar goal in their business in one month's time? Do your colleagues or competitors who have been in business about the same length of time routinely get that much business? If so, you have set a realistic goal, no matter how unattainable it may seem to you right now.

If any of these tests makes you fear that the goal you have set is unrealistic, change it now. There's no fun, and even less value, in struggling to meet a goal that was never achievable in the first place.

One final hint: If you are just starting out in business, you might consider setting a goal based on a certain number of leads acquired, prospects con-

"When you are reaching for an important new goal, watch out for the Impostor Syndrome. Even when you know that taking risks is essential to your success, you may still feel awkward in new situations. You know you need to stretch yourself, but when you push beyond your comfort zone, you can feel uncomfortable and vulnerable. Psychologists label this fear the Impostor Syndrome.

"The symptoms are a fear of not being good enough, skilled enough, knowledgeable enough, or experienced enough—and, even worse, being found out. When you are suffering from this syndrome, you lack confidence, even if your qualifications and education are outstanding. You can find yourself obsessively overcompensating for your perceived deficits.

"Successful people learn to go ahead even when they feel like impostors, knowing that they will gain confidence and whatever else is required along the way. Realizing that this syndrome is a natural part of new undertakings may help it seem less awkward. Trust your abilities; you have what it takes to succeed. Your self-confidence just hasn't caught up yet."

Pamela Gilberd, speaker and author of *The Eleven Commandments of Wildly Successful Women* (Macmillan Spectrum, 1996)

tacted, or presentations given rather than closed sales. Remember the length of the marketing cycle for our management systems consultant in the previous chapter. If you are starting from scratch to fill your pipeline, closing a sale in the next 28 days might be out of reach for you.

## Are You Resisting This Process?

Have you read this entire discussion of goal setting without yet setting a goal? Or did you choose one but tell yourself, "I don't have to set a real goal. This is just an exercise"? It's time to ask yourself why. Or better yet, what is in the way?

Are you afraid? Of what? Failing? Succeeding? Offending someone? Looking silly? Do you have some negative past experience with goal setting that is causing you to avoid it? Whatever it is that is preventing you from choosing a real honest-to-goodness, no-kidding, I-can-do-this goal, get it out in the open now. This program will not work for you unless you set a realistic goal.

Write out your fears and concerns, draw or paint them, talk them out with your business buddy, action group, personal coach, or a friend. Do whatever it takes to discover what is stopping you, and then stop letting it stop you. Make a conscious choice to try goal setting one more time, or for the first time. Trust the process. It works.

## Locking It In

Great work! Now that you have a goal, find someone to tell it to. If you are working with a buddy, group, or coach, you already have a place to share your goal. If not, tell it to a friend or colleague. Stating goals out loud grants them more reality than just writing them down. And telling someone else what you plan to accomplish creates a sense of accountability on your part to give you an extra push toward that goal.

# Part II

## The System

| Chapter | 4 |
| --- | --- |

# What's Stopping You?
# Selecting Your
# Success Ingredients

*Security is mostly a superstition. Life is either a daring adventure or nothing. . . . Avoiding danger is no safer in the long run than outright exposure.*

—Helen Keller

With a realistic goal in place, you are now ready to take the next step in designing the action plan you will follow for the next month. You will be selecting your success ingredients—the missing ingredients you need in order to be successful.

## What Are the Missing Ingredients?

Success ingredients are the tools, information, or skills you need to address successfully the "stuck" area you have uncovered in your marketing. Each stage of the universal marketing cycle requires a different list of key ingredients for effective marketing. If you are working on filling the pipeline, for example, you may need to find some networking events to attend. But if your focus is on closing sales, this ingredient won't be helpful. You might need instead to design a good selling script.

The place to begin in choosing success ingredients is to ask yourself why you are not moving forward in your chosen stage of the universal marketing cycle. "Why can't I fill the pipeline?" you might ask. Or, "Why aren't I following up?" Your answer might point you to a needed success ingredient right away. Stop and think about this: what tools, information, or skills are you missing to help you fill the pipeline, follow up, get presentations, or close sales?

## Shopping for Success Ingredients

In the design of your Get Clients Now! program, you should have at least one, and no more than three, success ingredients that you plan to work on over the next month. To help you select just the right ingredients for your plan, a success ingredient shopping list appears in Figure 4-1.

In reviewing the shopping list, it is important that you look at only the section that applies to your chosen marketing stage. Don't overwhelm yourself by checking out all the other options. You have already determined exactly where you need to focus right now, so stay with it. If you are ready to move on to another stage by the next time you use the program, that will be time enough to look at the other possibilities.

Some of the terms on the shopping list may be unfamiliar. To help you decide which are the right ingredients for you, see the guide in Figure 4-2. Don't worry about the how-tos of acquiring and employing the ingredients right now. Once you have chosen which ones you will use, you will find more information about them in the detailed marketing recipes in Part III ("The Strategies") of this book.

To the left of each ingredient in Figure 4-1 is an icon that identifies which of the six marketing strategies that ingredient is used for. (The icons are reviewed for your convenience on page 51.) Some ingredients, such as "description of services" and "business cards," have all of the icons because they are tools that can be used with any of the strategies. The others are marked with the one or two icons that represent the strategies that each specific ingredient supports.

The best way to use the shopping list is as an idea generator rather than a prescription. You probably already know better than anyone else what ingredients you are missing in your marketing. As you read through the list, keep asking yourself why you can't be or aren't being successful in your stuck area. Place a check mark next to each ingredient you suspect might be missing for you.

## Editing Your Shopping List

If you came up with three success ingredients or fewer, you may be done! If you selected more than three, it's time to prioritize. To make sure you are choosing the most important ingredients, take a look at the marketing strategies you have decided to use. Since you will be using only those strategies for the present, you should eliminate any ingredients that you don't actually need to implement your chosen strategies. For example, if you are working on filling the pipeline but did not choose writing and publicity as one of your strategies,

**The Strategy Icons**

 Direct contact and follow-up

 Networking and referral building

 Public speaking

 Writing and publicity

 Promotional events

 Advertising

you should not be selecting publicity venues, press release or kit, or letter to the editor as success ingredients, no matter how attractive they sound. You have spent quite a bit of effort already in diagnosing your stuck area and picking the right strategies to address it, so don't second-guess yourself now.

(Text continues on page 58.)

**Figure 4-1. Success ingredient shopping list.**

To fill the pipeline . . .

- Description of services
- Target market definition
- 10-second introduction
- Business cards
- Prospect list
- Lead sources
- Networking venues
- Referral partners
- Networking skills
- Speaking venues
- Speaking topics
- Speaker's bio
- Writing venues
- Writing query
- Publicity venues
- Press release or kit
- Letter to the editor
- Promotion concept
- Promotion plan
- Web site
- Web registrations or links
- Advertising venues
- Flyer venues
- Ad copy, layout, or script

To follow up more effectively . . .

- Brochure
- Marketing kit
- Model marketing letters
- Contact management system
- Computer
- Personal mailing list
- Postcard or mailer
- Newsletter
- E-mail address
- 30-second commercial

To turn more contacts into presentations . . .

- Telephone script
- Telemarketing skills
- Qualifying questions
- Higher-quality leads and referrals
- Professional visibility
- Competitive research
- Target market research
- New market position
- Better service package
- Narrower focus of services

To turn more presentations into sales . . .

- Better-qualified prospects
- Presentation script
- Presentation visuals
- Presentation skills
- Selling script
- Selling skills
- Portfolio
- Leave-behind
- Professional credibility
- Testimonials or references

**Figure 4-2. Success ingredient guide.**

*Filling the Pipeline*

• *Description of services.* A clear oral and written description of the features, benefits, structure, and cost of your services.

• *Target market definition.* Description of the specific market or markets you will target with your marketing. Base your description on demographics or industry classifications rather than their presumed need for you.

• *10-second introduction.* Self-introduction that describes what you do and who you do it for in a clear and memorable way.

• *Business cards.* To be effective, they must specifically state what you do, but not contain a laundry list of your talents. Don't list multiple businesses on the same card.

• *Prospect list.* List of people or companies that fit your target market definition. You can buy one or create your own through networking, referrals, speaking, and other avenues.

• *Lead sources.* Groups, events, institutions, publications, or other media that can give you information about potential clients on a regular basis.

• *Networking venues.* Places, groups, and events where you can meet prospective clients and referral partners.

• *Referral partners.* People, groups, or institutions that are willing to refer potential clients to you.

• *Networking skills.* Techniques or experience you need to feel more comfortable about networking. You might read a book, take a workshop, or practice with friends.

• *Speaking venues.* Places, groups, or events where you might be able to speak to promote your business.

• *Speaking topics.* Description of one to three topics you are available to speak on to groups of prospective clients or referral partners.

• *Speaker's bio.* Description of your background and experience that you send to potential speaking venues to pique their interest.

• *Writing venues.* Publications for which you can write expert articles or an ongoing column.

• *Writing query.* Inquiry to a potential writing venue, describing a topic you would like to write about. Some venues want to see a finished article; most prefer that you send a query letter before writing.

• *Publicity venues.* Media you can approach to get quoted, interviewed, or profiled.

• *Press release or kit.* A release is a bulletin you send to the media to get press coverage. In some cases, it may be accompanied by a marketing kit (defined below), and is then called a press kit.

• *Letter to the editor.* Letter you write to editors and producers to make them aware of your expertise. Usually written in response to a published or broadcast piece.

• *Promotion concept.* Idea for a promotional event or trade show display.

• *Promotion plan.* Plan for producing an event or appearance at a show.

• *Web site.* Site on the World Wide Web where others can find out about your services, sample your expertise, or communicate with you.

• *Web registrations or links.* A way for people to find your site. Registrations with search engines and links from other web sites are the two best ways to increase traffic to your site.

• *Advertising venues.* Media you can advertise in to reach your target market: newspapers, magazines, newsletters, trade journals, directories, radio, or TV.

• *Flyer venues.* Places where you can post, distribute, or circulate a flyer.

• *Ad copy, layout, or script.* What your proposed ad will say and how it will look.

### Following Up

• *Brochure.* May be simple and inexpensive or deluxe and very pricey. Think of it primarily as a follow-up tool rather than for filling the pipeline.

• *Marketing kit.* Replaces a brochure when you are proposing big-ticket business. Includes several pieces (e.g., description of services, professional bio, client list, testimonials, or articles).

• *Model marketing letters.* Boilerplate you pick and choose from to create letters you send to contacts rather than writing each one from scratch. Can even replace a brochure.

• *Contact management system.* Method of keeping track of all your contacts. Could be 3- by 5-inch cards, a notebook, or a computer system (usually with some information on paper as well).

• *Computer.* If you are managing more than 300 contacts, you need a computer-based contact management system. Having all your marketing literature on a computer also allows you to revise and customize it on the fly.

• *Personal mailing list.* An essential tool for follow-up. The best kind is one you generate yourself while filling the pipeline. May also be acquired from groups or events where you have already made contact.

• *Postcard or mailer.* A piece of literature you send to your mailing list to remind contacts that you are still around.

*(Continues)*

**Figure 4-2 continued.**

---

• *Newsletter.* A way to demonstrate your expertise and follow up at the same time. Can be in print and sent by regular mail, or a text-only version you fax or send by e-mail.

• *E-mail address.* For prospective clients who prefer this mode of communication, it may be the only way to reach them. It is also much cheaper than using regular mail.

• *30-second commercial.* What you leave on someone's voice mail when you call to follow up and the person isn't in. Also useful in networking groups and when meeting a potential client in person for the first time.

### Getting Presentations

• *Telephone script.* What you say when you make cold calls, warm calls, and follow-up calls. Usually includes an attention-grabbing phrase and answers to common objections.

• *Telemarketing skills.* Techniques or experience you need to improve your telephone presence. You might read a book, listen to a tape, take a workshop, or practice more.

• *Qualifying questions.* Questions you ask up front to determine whether someone is a good prospect for your service. Only qualified prospects are worth your time and effort to follow up with.

• *Higher-quality leads and referrals.* The prospects who are most likely to buy, based on their demographic or industry profile, or the source of the original lead. If you develop a profile of your best potential customers, you can seek out more leads that fit the profile.

• *Professional visibility.* Making yourself more visible in your professional community will increase the likelihood that prospects know your name before you contact them. Using the influence of the know-like-and-trust factor in this way will secure you more presentations.

• *Competitive research.* Information about the competition that enables you to better compete. When you know what clients like about your competitors, you can emulate it. When you know what clients dislike, you can inform your prospects how you are superior.

• *Target market research.* Information about your prospective clients that tells you more about what they want. Research can lead to finding a new market, or help determine which of many targets is the best one to pursue.

• *New market position.* Your market position is how prospects think of you in comparison to your competitors. If prospects aren't seeing you as just right for them, you can change your positioning to make them view you differently.

- *Better service package.* A different way of packaging your services to make them more attractive to prospective clients. It might entail changing how you set or charge fees, bundling different services together, or including products in your package.

- *Narrower focus of services.* Limiting what you present or propose to the one or two lines of business that your prospects are most likely to buy. A narrower focus will allow prospects to better grasp what you have to offer.

### Closing Sales

- *Better-qualified prospects.* If your presentations aren't turning into sales, this is the first place to look. Refer to "Qualifying questions" and "Higher-quality leads and referrals" above to see how you might find better prospects to present to.

- *Presentation script.* An outline of what you plan to present. Include the questions you need to ask, everything you want to be sure to say, and responses to the questions you might get.

- *Presentation visuals.* Something for the client to look at that will make your service more tangible, such as a diagram of your process.

- *Presentation skills.* Techniques or experience you need to get more comfortable at presenting. You might take a workshop, work with a coach, or join a group to practice.

- *Selling script.* A list of important points to remember when selling. Your script should include closing-the-sale questions and answers to common objections.

- *Selling skills.* Techniques or experience you need to do a better job at closing the sale. Books, tapes, workshops, and role play can be helpful.

- *Portfolio.* Tangible examples of your work that you can show to a prospect. Case studies, photographs, and samples of writing or reports can all help to make a sale.

- *Leave-behind.* Something extra you leave with the client to look over after your presentation. It reminds the client of you and gives you a great reason to follow up soon.

- *Professional credibility.* Increasing your credibility will cut down on questions about your background and experience. You may need to more clearly emphasize your credentials in your presentation, or work on acquiring better credentials to present.

- *Testimonials or references.* Letters or quotes from satisfied customers, or a list of impressive references, with their contact information.

If you eliminate those distractions and still have more than three success ingredients, ask yourself which three you need first. During the month of your program, you will be acquiring or creating the ingredients you choose. As you complete your first choices, you can cross them off the list and start work on others.

Let's say you are focusing on following up and are considering working on a brochure, model marketing letters, a contact management system, and a newsletter. It would make more sense to begin with the first three, since the brochure, model marketing letters, and contact management system would all help you follow up with hot prospects; the newsletter would be more typically used with cool or stale ones. If you complete any one of the three within the month, you could then start work on the newsletter.

The success ingredients you choose don't necessarily need to be completed within one month; you are just deciding to work on them over the next month. A 30-second commercial is something you might knock off in a couple of hours, but creating a brochure might take you six weeks from start to finish.

If you're still not sure which ingredients you should choose, skip to Part III, which has a chapter for each stage of the universal marketing cycle. See what the chapter for your chosen stage has to say about the success ingredients you are considering, and then pick no more than three to start with.

## Setting Target Completion Dates

It's time to record those success ingredients on your action worksheet. Look at the example in Figure 4-3. List the ingredients you have chosen on the success ingredients section of your own worksheet; notice that the example shows target dates for each one. You need to do this too, so think about what would be a realistic amount of time to allow yourself to complete or acquire each item. It's okay to choose a target date that is more than a month away.

In setting a target date for your success ingredients, use the guidelines introduced in Chapter 3 for realistic goal setting. Review the "Time for a Reality Check" section if you need a refresher. You should consider both the actual time and the elapsed time needed for completion.

If you decided you were finally going to finish that brochure you've been working on, it might take you only two hours to complete a final review of the last draft your graphic designer sent you. But then it will take the designer time to make your changes and get it to the printer, and the printer will need time to get it on the press. So estimate how much elapsed time will be required to get it all done.

If you aren't sure, don't leave the target date blank while you check with the designer and the printer to see what is reasonable. Allowing others to determine your schedule may be one of the habits that has gotten you into trouble in the

"Finding space in your busy life for a big project like developing a brochure can be a challenge," says Caterina Rando, success coach and professional speaker. "Sometimes we have so much to do that we feel paralyzed. When that happens, write down everything you think you need to do. Decide what is urgent, and what you can put off. Ask yourself if there is anything you can forget about doing, and if there's anything that someone else can do.

"Try working in increments. Tell yourself you will give yourself a break in an hour. Psychologically, you will feel more at ease with the situation. At the end of the hour, take a break, even if it is just a walk down the hall. This is also good for the creative process; it gives your conscious mind an opportunity to wander and come up with some new ideas.

"If you are really dreading doing something, find a way to make it fun. I always pay my bills while watching a *Star Trek* rerun; that makes it tolerable. I have a client who returns all possible phone calls from her Jacuzzi early in the morning. Play upbeat music when working in your office.

"Break down your project into bite-size chunks. I used to tell myself that I would take a whole day and do nothing else but clean my office. I never did it, because the idea was too dreadful. Instead, what I do now is work on it in 15-minute segments.

"I often procrastinate when I need to do some writing. The mental block that is in my way is that I believe or feel that I don't know how to say what I want to say. But if I sit down and start tapping on the keyboard, it will work itself out. So don't sit around wondering how you might get it done. Simply start to do it and see what happens."

Caterina Rando, Certified Professional and Personal Coach
and speaker, www.CaterinaR.com

past. Try this instead: decide when you would like to have the printed brochure in your hand; then call the designer and say, "I need to have my brochure complete by the 31st. If I get you my final changes by the 20th, can you meet that date?" If your request is unreasonable, the designer will tell you. Then you can negotiate for a new date, and change the target date on your worksheet.

The function of having a target date for each success ingredient, just like setting a marketing goal, is to get you into action immediately. Once your brochure has a due date, you will make a call about it and say, "This is when

**Figure 4-3. Adding success ingredients to the action worksheet.**

## *GET CLIENTS NOW!*™ Action Worksheet

What strategies will you use?

| 1. DIRECT CONTACT AND FOLLOW-UP | 2. NETWORKING AND REFERRAL BUILDING | 3. PUBLIC SPEAKING | 4. WRITING AND PUBLICITY | 5. PROMOTIONAL EVENTS | 6. ADVERTISING |
|---|---|---|---|---|---|
| ☑ | ☑ | ☐ | ☐ | ☐ | ☐ |

Where are you stuck?  ☑ Filling the pipeline  ☐ Following up  ☐ Getting presentations  ☐ Closing sales

How much business do you have now?  _11 clients_

How much business do you *really* want?  _20 clients_

What would that get you?  _pay off my credit cards, take a vacation, feel less stressed_

What is your program goal?  _4 new clients by the end of the program_

What will be your reward?  _go on a ski weekend_

| Success Ingredients | Target Date |
|---|---|
| 1. target market definition | 9/17/99 |
| 2. 10-second introduction | 9/24/99 |
| 3. 8 networking venues | 10/1/99 |

Daily Actions

1. _____
2. _____
3. _____
4. _____
5. _____
6. _____
7. _____
8. _____
9. _____
10. _____

Special Permission _____

I need it," instead of, "When can you have it?" You will immediately be in more control of your marketing, and much more likely to produce results sooner.

Changing the target date later on is not cheating. It is being realistic. What is the point of beating yourself up because you didn't meet a target date that you already knew was impossible? Since this is our second look at goal setting, and we will be using these techniques over and over in the program, let's take a moment to examine the core philosophy of this process.

### Get Clients Now! Goal-Setting Philosophy

1. Set a goal that will stretch you, but that you believe is realistic.

2. Try your best to meet it.

3. When your goal becomes unrealistic, change it.

4. Reward yourself for effort, not just results.

Point 4 is a key element of the process. Marketing is unpredictable. Sometimes you do everything exactly right, and still don't get the results you want when you want them. If you reward yourself only when you get results, all the hard work that led up to the result often gets discounted. And in the meantime, you feel as if you aren't getting anywhere.

Get into the habit of rewarding yourself for effort, regardless of your results. To do this consistently, you will always need a goal. If you decide, for example, that you will make 10 follow-up calls on Monday, and you make them, you deserve some acknowledgment even if none of those people wanted to buy today. This strategy is particularly important where success ingredients are concerned. Having a brochure may be crucial for the success of your business, but the brochure alone will not get you any clients. You will need to call, mail, and so forth, before that brochure turns into sales. Therefore you need to reward yourself up front for all the effort that went into completing the brochure.

Returning to the task of setting target dates for success ingredients, you may be puzzled about what to do if your success ingredient is a skill set instead of something tangible. Let's say that you want to improve your networking skills. To set a target date for that, imagine that you are scoring yourself on a scale of 0 to 100 percent. If 0 percent means you can't network at all and 100 percent means you are a star networker, what would be your score today? If you set the final day of your 28-day program as your target date for this ingredient, what would you like your score to be then? That's the answer you write on your worksheet, for example, "networking skills at 75 percent."

You can use this same scoring technique to set targets for other intangible success ingredients like professional credibility or better service package. Just

Robert Middleton is a marketing consultant who helps service businesses attract clients. The following is an excerpt from his e-mail newsletter, *Marketing Flash!* It was written just after the sudden death of Princess Diana.

"If you're at all like me, this tragedy may have been like a wake-up call—a reminder of the impermanence and preciousness of life. But what does all of this have to do with marketing? If you look at marketing your business as the way to make your contribution real in the world, marketing is as important as life itself.

"Working with hundreds of businesspeople over the past 14 years, every one of them had a dream. A dream to make a difference, to make a contribution or to simply experience the deep satisfaction that comes from true accomplishment.

"And most of these clients saw marketing as a barrier—a hurdle they needed to master before they could realize their dreams. In most cases this hurdle was learning an important marketing skill such as networking, giving presentations, writing a letter or brochure, or making that dreaded cold call.

"In many cases, the biggest barrier was fear. Fear of failure, fear of rejection, or fear of taking a risk. And the only thing that kept them going was that dream—the awareness that if they didn't make the effort to market their business, their dreams might end up on the trash heap.

"Life is short. Will you reach your dreams? Will you make the contribution you could? Will you overcome your resistance and fears in pursuit of your goals?

"... Will you take every opportunity to master yourself in order to realize your highest ideals? Will you work with more passion, with more joy?

"... Will you let go of complaint and excuses? Will you start making the effort to do what is difficult, yet deeply rewarding?

"... Will you make that extra call, work the extra hours, go the extra mile, do what you think is literally impossible?

"... Will you dig deeper into your creative resources and emerge with ideas and solutions that can make a difference in the lives of your clients?

"Life is short.... Don't waste it. Market your business (and work at your business) as if it mattered as much as life itself. It does."

Robert Middleton, marketing consultant,
Action Plan Marketing, www.actionplan.com

make the target completion date the day your program will end, and decide what score you would like to achieve by then. If this seems arbitrary, it is. But you are the only one who can accurately judge your own progress. The goal, and your progress toward it, has to make sense and feel good to you. That's the only way a goal can work its motivation magic.

Your success ingredient might be an item that requires some quantification in order to be specific enough to serve as a goal. If you chose writing venues, for example, how many is enough? Pick a number that would make you feel as if you had really satisfied that need for a while, and write it on your worksheet—for example, "10 writing venues" or "3 testimonials."

Once you have chosen at least one but no more than three success ingredients, written them on your action worksheet, assigned target dates to them, and made them specific in terms of number needed or scores you wish to achieve, you have completed four of the six steps in designing your program. In Chapter 5, you will be choosing the precise actions you will take to get clients over the next 28 days.

# Here's What to Do: Choosing From the Action Plan Menu

*We must not sit down and wait for miracles. Up, and be going!*
—John Eliot, seventeenth-century British missionary

The final, and most important, piece of designing your own personal Get Clients Now! program is to select the specific marketing and sales actions you plan to take on a regular basis over the next month. These are the actions that will generate business for you.

### Where Do the Clients Come From?

In the introduction to this book, you learned the most important secret of service business marketing and sales: The magic formula is choosing a set of simple, effective things to do, and doing them consistently. That's where the clients come from.

You are about to do exactly this. You are going to choose 10 specific actions to take, and perform them daily or weekly for the next 28 days. Your choosing will be based on the "stuck place" you uncovered with the universal marketing cycle and the marketing strategies you selected to address that stuck place. But it is your doing of those actions that will get you the clients.

There is an interesting phenomenon that occurs when you get serious about marketing in a focused, consistent way. You begin to get results in unexpected places. The telephone rings, and it's a prospect you spoke to three months ago saying he is suddenly interested in working with you. You go to a networking meeting that seems like a complete waste of time while you are there, and run into a hot new prospect in the elevator on your way out. You get an exciting referral from someone whose name you don't even recognize. It's almost as if the universe has noticed how hard you are working and decided to reward you.

Don't make the mistake of thinking that these out-of-the-blue opportunities are accidents. There is a direct connection between the level of effort you put into marketing and the results you get out of it, even when it seems as if the results are completely unrelated to your efforts.

This phenomenon is so common with people who use the Get Clients Now! program that it has a name: the *persistence effect*. If you persist in making 10 calls a day, every day, you will get business, but it won't all come from the calls you made. If you consistently attend one networking event per week, clients will appear, but not necessarily from the events you attended. Don't worry about why it works; just know that it works.

The existence of the persistence effect can help you enormously in choosing the daily actions for your program, because there is another secret to successful service business marketing: It doesn't matter so much *what* you choose as *that* you choose.

Picking 10 things you can do, and doing them, will break you out of analysis paralysis, give you a plan, and get you into action. Even if you picked the wrong 10 things, the persistence effect would make this focused activity pay off for you. Would it pay off as well as picking the right 10 things? Probably not. And that's why you are going to choose only actions that represent the stage of the marketing cycle you are focusing on and the marketing strategies you already selected.

## Ordering From the Action Plan Menu

There are two ways of going about selecting what daily actions to include in your program. One way is to choose from the selections already prepared for you that appear on the action plan menu (see Figure 5-1 later in this section). The other is to design your own unique actions. Let's look first at designing your own.

Suppose you are focusing on closing sales, and you have chosen direct contact and follow-up as one of your marketing strategies. How could you use this strategy to close more sales? Perhaps you could follow up better by recontacting people you have already presented to but didn't buy from you at the time. To turn this into a specific, consistent action, give it a time frame and quantify it—for example, "Follow up with five prospects who didn't buy each week."

How do you know how often to do something and how much of it to do? You guess. How much activity do you think will be necessary to achieve the result you want? How much do you have time for? The right answer is proba-

Josiane Feigon specializes in training and consulting with professionals and entrepreneurs to be more effective in selling and servicing customers over the phone. "In terms of marketing," says Josiane, "I walk my talk every day. I have built my entire client base through making cold calls to prospects over the phone. I have won all of my business because my customers say, 'If she sounds this effective by phone, I would like her to work with my team.'

"My company grew very fast from the beginning and was always difficult to keep up with. However, there came a time when it stopped as quickly as it started. Most of that was due to the lack of regular marketing on my part. I thought if I could just manage my clients and answer incoming calls, that would get me through the day, but I was not taking a step back to plan and look ahead at the next step. Overnight, everything dried up; all my current contracts came to an end, everyone was reviewing their budget at the same time, and all my bills came in.

"I used the Get Clients Now! system to get back on track and design a plan for myself. I kept a copy of it in front of me at all times during the week. My slump didn't feel so empty as I started to work proactively versus working reactively."

Here are Josiane's tips for entrepreneurs who are managing service businesses:

• Constantly feed the marketing part of your business, and do not ignore it.

• Design a maintenance strategy for your busy times and a prospecting strategy for slower times.

• Never refuse to take on new business for fear of not managing it properly; it always works out in the long run.

• Use the slump times to plan and reinvent areas of your business that are growing stale.

• When people ask you how your business is doing, always say, "It's doing great!"

Josiane Feigon, telemarketing
trainer, consultant, and coach,
TeleSmart Communications,
www.tele-smart.com

bly somewhere between those two. But really, there is no right answer. It does-
n't matter so much what you choose as that you choose.

Remember the Get Clients Now! goal-setting philosophy:

1. Set a goal that will stretch you but that you believe is realistic.

2. Try your best to meet it.

3. When your goal becomes unrealistic, change it.

4. Reward yourself for effort, not just results.

You're going to use these same principles again in designing your daily
actions. Pick a time frame and quantity that seem to make sense. Try it out. If
it's not working, change it. And reward yourself for what you did, not what
you got.

You can choose to perform an action daily, weekly, or several times per
week. "Daily" typically means five days per week, which is the recommended
schedule for the Get Clients Now! program. The only rule is that all actions
must be performed at least weekly, because you need to develop consistency
in your marketing in order for the persistence effect to work. While it's okay to
change the frequency of your actions once you start the program, it's generally
not a good idea to change the actions themselves until you are ready to move
forward in the universal marketing cycle.

---

"People often get overwhelmed with all the things they 'could'
or 'should' be doing to market their business," observes career
and life planning coach Sarah Sharman. Sarah uses the Get
Clients Now! system with her clients who are making the shift
from corporate employee to self-employment. "I tell them the
story of when I was 25, and got my first few paychecks from
my first corporate job. The money was twice as much as I had
been making before. I was worried about how much money I
could afford to spend and how much I should be saving. My
dad said, 'Sarah, just save 10 percent of your paycheck, and
you can do what you want with the rest.' What a relief!

"Get Clients Now! works just like that. I tell my clients that
once they do the activities listed on their tracking worksheet,
the rest of their time is theirs to do what they want: have fun,
read a book, take a class, spend time with their family, whatever. This really frees them up, and gives them permission to
have a life even though they are starting a business."

Sarah Sharman, Certified
Professional and Personal Coach

Now that you know how the process of designing a daily action works, take a look at the action plan menu in Figure 5-1. The menu is divided into three sections:

*Appetizers*—actions that will help you to create or acquire success ingredients
*Main course*—actions focused directly on getting business
*Dessert*—actions to help you be more effective and productive in general

You are going to choose 10 daily actions, either from the menu or of your own design. As with a meal, you will need to balance your selections. The best combination for a satisfying marketing banquet is one or two actions from the appetizer menu, seven or eight main courses, and one dessert. This design will create an effective balance between project work (e.g., building a web site), actual business development (e.g., making cold calls), and self-management (e.g, getting enough sleep) in your action plan.

## Start With the Fun Stuff

In a few pages, you will be choosing your main course selections—those actions that will directly get you business. It's a good bet that the process of making those choices may bring up some fear and resistance for you, so let's start with the fun stuff—appetizers and dessert.

*Appetizers* are action items to move you forward in the process of creating or acquiring your chosen success ingredients. By putting one or two appetizers on your list of daily actions, you are making a commitment to do what it takes to get those missing ingredients in place. If you chose only one success ingredient, you probably only need one appetizer, but with two or three ingredients to create, you may want two appetizers to help you along.

The appetizers on the action plan menu are suggested actions for you to choose from, but you can also design your own. Remember that the time frame and quantity are up to you in either case. Here are some ways you can use the ones on the menu:

• *Spend 1 hour each day on my success ingredient project.* Good for projects like lead sources or publicity venues that may take awhile to ferret out.

• *Complete 1 item on my success ingredient project list each day.* Use this for projects such as a contact management system or portfolio, where you may have a list of many steps to getting it done.

• *Practice my skills or a script once per day.* An excellent choice for ingredients like a telephone script or negotiating skills, where you need to practice to make progress.

*(Text continues on page 73.)*

**Figure 5-1. Action plan menu.**

**Appetizers:** *Choose 1 or 2*

*To create success ingredients ...*

Spend 1 hour each day on my success ingredient project.

Complete 1 item on my success ingredient project list each day.

Practice my skills or script once per day.

Spend 1 hour each week doing research.

Read or write 1 hour every day.

Interview 1 person per week.

Collect 1 new fact per day.

Observe how it's done once per week.

**Main Course:** *Choose 7 or 8*

*To fill the pipeline by attracting more prospects ...*

 Send a mailing to 10 new people each week.

Distribute or post 10 flyers weekly.

Post 1 on-line bulletin board notice weekly.

Introduce myself in front of a group once per week.

Volunteer in a visible position once per week.

Do 1 thing to get my name in print each week.

*To fill the pipeline by making more contacts ...*

 Meet 20 new people in my target market each week.

Go to 1 networking event each week.

Spend 1 hour each day cold-calling.

Call 1 new person per day.

Contact 3 groups or associations each week about speaking.

Speak to 1 group or association each week.

*To fill the pipeline by gathering more leads ...*

 Read 1 trade paper or journal each week.

Review 5 pages of an advertising or professional directory daily.

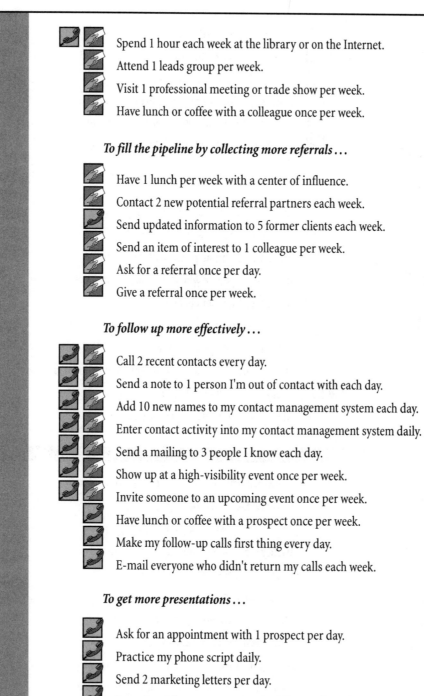

Spend 1 hour each week at the library or on the Internet.

Attend 1 leads group per week.

Visit 1 professional meeting or trade show per week.

Have lunch or coffee with a colleague once per week.

### To fill the pipeline by collecting more referrals ...

Have 1 lunch per week with a center of influence.

Contact 2 new potential referral partners each week.

Send updated information to 5 former clients each week.

Send an item of interest to 1 colleague per week.

Ask for a referral once per day.

Give a referral once per week.

### To follow up more effectively ...

Call 2 recent contacts every day.

Send a note to 1 person I'm out of contact with each day.

Add 10 new names to my contact management system each day.

Enter contact activity into my contact management system daily.

Send a mailing to 3 people I know each day.

Show up at a high-visibility event once per week.

Invite someone to an upcoming event once per week.

Have lunch or coffee with a prospect once per week.

Make my follow-up calls first thing every day.

E-mail everyone who didn't return my calls each week.

### To get more presentations ...

Ask for an appointment with 1 prospect per day.

Practice my phone script daily.

Send 2 marketing letters per day.

Interview 1 former or prospective client each week.

*(Continues)*

**Figure 5-1 continued.**

Solicit 1 testimonial each week.

Research 1 competitor each week.

Meet with 1 new referral partner each week.

Follow up with 3 potential referral partners weekly.

Volunteer for a high-profile organization once per week.

Make 2 queries about speaking each week.

*To close more sales...*

Call all prospects back within 7 days.

Get 10 noes each week.

Make 1 challenging phone call every day.

Recontact 3 people who didn't buy, every week.

Recontact 1 former client each day.

Practice selling to the mirror every day.

Attend 1 high-profile event weekly.

Have 2 lunches per week with centers of influence.

Speak to an influential group once per week.

Make 1 article-writing query each week.

**Dessert:** *Choose 1*

*To be more effective in everything I do...*

Plan my day each morning.

Do all my "A-list" tasks first each day.

Write in my success journal each evening.

Exercise 3 times per week.

Get 8 hours of sleep every night.

Meditate for 1/2 hour per day.

Schedule a day of fun each week.

Add up my income and expenses each week.

Spend 1/2 hour each day organizing my office.

Visualize success daily.

- *Spend 1 hour each week doing research.* Appropriate for ingredients such as speaking venues or competitive research.

- *Read or write 1 hour every day.* Use this for information-gathering projects like finding the right advertising venues, or creative work such as writing to increase your professional credibility.

- *Interview 1 person per week.* Good for projects such as researching your target market or discovering how to qualify your prospects better.

- *Collect 1 new fact per day.* Another method of quantifying your progress in research or information gathering.

- *Observe how it's done once per week.* A great way to improve your skills in areas like networking or selling.

When you have chosen one or two appetizers, write them down as the first two daily actions on your action worksheet (see Figure 5-2 for an example).

Next, look at the *dessert* selections. The daily actions on the dessert menu are suggested ways in which you can be more effective and productive in everything you do. Choose just one. To make the right choice, ask yourself what is likely to get in the way of your success this month. Have you identified any habits or behavior that tend to sabotage you? Is there something you need to do for yourself to perform at your best?

Use these descriptions of the dessert selections on the action plan menu to help you choose one or design your own:

- *Plan my day each morning.* If you often come to the end of the day and wonder where it went, this dessert may be a good choice for you. Planning your day in advance will take only 5 or 10 minutes. You could also make your plan the night before.

- *Do all my "A-list" tasks first each day.* Not everything on your personal to-do list is of equal value. Try giving every item on the list a priority of A, B, or C, and then take care of all the A's first each day.

- *Write in my success journal each evening.* It's easy to get caught up in failures and shortcomings, but every day has successes in it. Start a success journal, where you write only those things you enjoyed, got recognition for, or felt good about accomplishing each day.

- *Exercise 3 times per week.* If you find that regular exercise gives you more energy, it may be just as important to effective marketing as a good telephone script.

- *Get 8 hours of sleep every night.* Depriving yourself of sleep is not good time management and will backfire quickly. Not everyone needs eight hours, so substitute the right number for your needs.

• *Meditate for 1/2 hour per day.* Meditation, drawing or painting, gardening, and needlework are four of the many avenues to reserve time for relaxation and quiet reflection. Just plain wool gathering is fine too. The idea is to give your overworked brain a rest.

• *Schedule a day of fun each week.* Relaxation takes many forms, and you may need some pleasurable activity more than a rest. Scheduling it in advance will make sure it happens.

• *Add up my income and expenses each week.* Think of this as a motivational technique. If you need to make another $300 this week, you may want to pick up the phone on Friday afternoon. If you see your hard work paying off, you may be inspired to do a little more.

• *Spend 1/2 hour each day organizing my office.* Keeping track of where each prospect is in the marketing cycle can be crucial to closing sales. Time spent looking for important papers that have gone missing is time you don't have available for marketing.

• *Visualize success daily.* This is a proved technique for improved achievement. Spend a few minutes each day seeing yourself succeeding at marketing, selling, and earning the rewards that are important to you. You may even want to do this three times a day.

After reading these descriptions, you may be tempted to choose more than one dessert. But you do need to leave enough room for the main course, so limit yourself to just one. If one of the desserts on the menu caused you to say, "That would really help me," that's the one to pick. And if you have a self-sabotaging habit that none of these addresses, make up your own dessert to help you start changing it.

Record your dessert as the last daily action on your action worksheet (see Figure 5-2).

## Time for the Main Course

The daily actions in the main course section of the menu are activities designed to get you clients. The main course items are grouped into categories that match the stages of the universal marketing cycle: filling the pipeline, following up, getting presentations, and closing sales. Because the possible activities for filling the pipeline are so varied, that area is subdivided into attracting prospects, making contacts, gathering leads, and collecting referrals.

You will be selecting seven or eight daily actions from the main course menu (or of your own design), to reach a total of 10 daily actions altogether. The first rule to follow in making your choices is this: Don't read the whole list! Look solely at the section that pertains to the marketing cycle stage you are working on.

**Figure 5-2. Adding daily actions to the action worksheet.**

## *GET CLIENTS NOW!*™ Action Worksheet

What strategies will you use?

| 1. DIRECT CONTACT AND FOLLOW-UP | 2. NETWORKING AND REFERRAL BUILDING | 3. PUBLIC SPEAKING | 4. WRITING AND PUBLICITY | 5. PROMOTIONAL EVENTS | 6. ADVERTISING |
|---|---|---|---|---|---|
| ☑ | ☑ | ☐ | ☐ | ☐ | ☐ |

Where are you stuck?   ☑ Filling the pipeline   ☐ Following up   ☐ Getting presentations   ☐ Closing sales

How much business do you have now?  _11 clients_

How much business do you *really* want?  _20 clients_

What would that get you?  _pay off my credit cards, take a vacation, feel less stressed_

What is your program goal?  _4 new clients by the end of the program_

What will be your reward?  _go on a ski weekend_

| Success Ingredients | Target Date |
|---|---|
| 1. _target market definition_ | _9/17/99_ |
| 2. _10-second introduction_ | _9/24/99_ |
| 3. _8 networking venues_ | _10/1/99_ |

Daily Actions

1. _Appetizer: spend 1/2 hour each day on my success ingredient projects_
2. _Main Course: introduce myself in front of a group once per week_
3. _Main Course: meet 20 new people in my target market each week_
4. _Main Course: go to 2 networking events each week_
5. _Main Course: have lunch with a colleague once per week_
6. _Main Course: call 1 new person per day_
7. _Main Course: contact 1 new potential referral partner each week_
8. _Main Course: send updated information to 3 former clients each week_
9. _Main Course: ask for a referral once per day_
10. _Dessert: visualize success daily_

Special Permission  _I give myself permission to have enough time for everything_

"There are many techniques for motivating yourself," declares Joyce Chapman, author of *Live Your Dream* (Newcastle Publishing, 1990), *Journaling for Joy* (Newcastle Publishing, 1991), and *If I Had Three Wishes, the Only One Would Be* (Newcastle Publishing, 1995). "One of the most effective methods is to ask someone to support you in living your dream. I know of a real estate salesman who promised to take his family camping every time he made a sale. His children became enthusiastic supporters of his success at work!"

Here are some of the other ways Joyce's clients have chosen to build more motivators into their everyday lives:

- Exercise daily.
- Put up notes around the house to remind myself to put first things (my dream) first.
- Treat myself to more walks on the beach.
- Set aside time each day just for myself.
- Play motivational tapes while I'm driving.
- Buy myself flowers.
- Plan minivacations to reward small milestones.

In Joyce's view, "Successful people do not spend a lot of time sitting around waiting for the phone to ring, for someone else to come and pump them up, or for the needed inspiration to carry on. Neither do they pretend they require no motivators and no support. They take charge, in this area as in others, of anticipating and providing for their own needs.

"Building motivators into your life is a powerful way of ensuring that your dream will receive the ongoing nourishment it needs, especially when the going gets tough, or you are under pressure or stress."

Joyce Chapman, author, speaker,
and coach, Live Your Dream,
www.joycechapman.com

On the left-hand side of the menu are the icons that tell you which of the six Get Clients Now! marketing strategies each activity is related to. For a key to the strategy icons, refer to Chapter 4. Some actions are applicable to only one strategy, while others could relate to several, depending on how they are used. There are two different approaches to making your selections:

1. *Just pick 'em.* As you have worked your way through the exercises in this book, you have already done a lot of thinking. You know where you are stuck in the marketing cycle, what marketing strategies you plan to use, and which are the missing ingredients for you to be successful. Maybe you don't need any more information than that to look at the daily actions listed for your marketing cycle stage and pick some. When you are ready to begin doing the actions you chose, you can read more about the tactics they represent in Part III.

2. *Understand the theory first.* Each daily action on the list represents an activity that has been proved effective in service business marketing. Sometimes the purpose of an activity will be immediately apparent. It's hard to mistake what "spend 1 hour each day cold calling" is about. But other activities are more subtle. For example, "Have 2 lunches per week with centers of influence" is listed under closing sales because this activity will simultaneously increase your visibility and credibility. When a prospective customer hears about you from someone she respects, it can greatly increase your likelihood of closing the sale.

If you want to understand more about the purpose of the main course activities before making your choices, read the chapter in Part III of this book that describes your chosen stage of the marketing cycle. You can skip any sections that relate to marketing strategies you will not be using.

Is one of these approaches to selecting main course actions more successful than the other? Actually, no. The difference is in you. If you are comfortable shooting from the hip, use approach 1. It's quicker and easier. If you don't like to commit to a course of action until you have thoroughly evaluated your choices, use approach 2. It will increase your level of commitment to the actions you choose.

## How to Make the Best Selections

Here are the questions you should ask yourself to make the best possible choices from the main course menu:

• *Where are you stuck?* You already know which stage of the universal marketing cycle you need to focus on, so choose only main course items that pertain to that stage. If you can't find seven or eight actions that seem right to you on the list for your stage, take one or two from the stage just before or after it, but don't skip around. Picking actions from several different stages will dilute your marketing efforts and sabotage the persistence effect.

• *Which marketing strategies are you using?* The icons shown for each action indicate what marketing strategy they relate to. Look for the actions that match up with the strategies you chose in Chapter 2. A large major-

Cynthia Loy Darst and Sherry Lowry are professional and personal coaches who advocate "marketing with heart. It's a non-traditional and highly gratifying approach to marketing versus sales, promotion, or advertising."

Cynthia and Sherry recommend that you make sure "all marketing activities are in line with your passion and vision. Vision sets the course—passion is the fire and the verve. They help you gain the courage and steam to build and maintain marketing momentum."

Some of their essentials for marketing with heart follow:

1. Know and use the gifts and talents that hold natural energy for you.

2. Find your "paths of least resistance" versus suffering, struggling, or muscling through.

3. Develop a truly "supportive" support system.

4. Let go of expectations of support, especially from family and friends who may experience change in your life as a threat to their own.

5. Triple your willingness and capacity to receive (or your marketing efforts can fail to stick).

6. People do business with those they know and trust. Get known!

7. Walk your talk.

8. Expect visits of fear and disillusionment; that's natural in an ever-changing business.

9. We attract the clients we are ready for. Learn fast and gratefully.

10. Persistence, patience, and consistency. Allow 18 to 36 months to develop a successful "heart-driven" business.

Cynthia Loy Darst, Certified Professional and
Personal Coach, www.TheCoaches.com/ctisch.htm
Sherry Lowry, personal development and business
coach, Lowry Group, www.sherrylowry.com

ity of the main course actions support the strategies of direct contact and follow-up and networking and referral building, because this is where the persistence effect has the most impact. If you want to include more actions that support some of the other strategies, feel free to make up some of your own. Remember, though, that you may have already chosen success ingredients that address those areas as well.

• *What will you actually do?* If you are paralyzed by cold calling or public speaking, there is no point in including these actions in your program, because you will simply avoid doing them. You might choose a success ingredient to help you improve your skills in these areas for the future, but the daily actions you pick need to be activities you are willing to do this month. Instead of choosing actions you could find immobilizing, ask yourself...

• *What are you naturally drawn to?* If you are typically outgoing and enjoy talking to people, choose actions that will get you to networking events and give you plenty of time on the phone. But if talking to strangers makes you so uncomfortable that you will do anything to avoid it, select actions that will allow you to concentrate on building referrals with people you already know or writing articles for publication. If you choose activities you like, or are at least willing to try, you will do them.

To make your selections, look at the section of the main course menu that corresponds to your stage of the marketing cycle. Place a check mark next to each daily action that seems to fit your situation. It's all right to pick one action (but only one) that is easy for you or that you are already doing consistently. You should also choose at least one that is really hard, and will stretch and challenge you.

If you end up with too many activities, ask yourself which would be the most efficient use of your time. What do you think will bring you the most return with the least effort? And remember: It doesn't matter so much what you choose as that you choose. Everything on the menu works.

When you have selected your 7 or 8 main course actions for a total of 10 daily actions overall, adjust the quantity and frequency of each one to suit you. Then write them on your action worksheet.

## A Word About Closing Sales

If you are working on filling the pipeline or following up, it may have occurred to you to wonder how you are actually going to make a sale. After all, the daily actions on your list are focused on the earlier stages in the cycle.

The key word to understanding the answer is *focus*. You have chosen to concentrate your effort on a particular stage of the marketing cycle because

"If you're not having any fun doing what you do, think back to a time when you were. What 'drudge' do you currently have that wasn't there when you were having fun? How can you eliminate the drudge when you are marketing your business?

"When you're not having any fun in your marketing, you are wasting your time, which just adds to the drudge. Don't you want to do business with people who seem to enjoy life and what they do for a living? If you wouldn't want to do business with yourself, you may be the problem in your marketing!

"If you can eliminate the drudge by having fun when you market yourself, you will draw to you the type of clients you really want."

Cat Williford, Certified Professional and Personal Coach

that is where you are feeling stuck. This doesn't mean, however, that you should ignore the routine functions of the other stages while you are doing this. If your pipeline-filling activities turn up a hot lead, follow up. If your follow-up generates a presentation, make it. If your presentation leads to closing the sale, great! That's what you want.

Your daily actions in the program are in no way intended to be everything you do about marketing and sales over the next month. You need to continue pursuing solid leads with the same energy you always have (or perhaps a little more, because now you have a goal to meet). The intent of the daily actions is simply to focus more effort on the area of your marketing that needs it the most.

The Get Clients Now! program should hold the same place in your marketing and sales activities as an exercise program does in your life. You don't quit walking to the bus stop because you are now doing 25 situps each morning, and you don't stop playing ball with the kids because you decide to run a mile three times a week. Regular life goes on while you are exercising; regular selling goes on while you are improving your performance in the areas of pipeline filling and follow-up.

## What Is Going to Stop You?

Look at what you have recorded on your action worksheet. You have an ambitious goal, success ingredients you are going to acquire or create, and a list of 10 daily actions you are going to perform, all in the next 28 days. If looking at this list makes you feel resistant, afraid, or overwhelmed, you are normal.

If you have ever attempted a program before—dieting or regular exercise, for example—or taken a motivational seminar, or made some New Year's res-

Tes Welborn, a dedicated user of the Get Clients Now! system, is a management consultant and business coach who regularly leads groups for consultants and professionals. Her advice: "You need to both market yourself—make your products and services visible—and sell your services—discuss with prospective clients their particular needs and the specific products and services that can meet those needs.

"People are often more comfortable with marketing—making themselves visible—than with sales—convincing others of their value and getting the contract. Yet to be successful, one must do both. The scarcity or uniqueness of the products and services you offer will determine the mix of marketing versus selling activities required. The more that your products and services are seen in the marketplace as common goods widely available, the greater the need for sales skills. The more that your products and services are seen as unique and valuable, the less critical sales skills become.

"The real secret to marketing and selling professional services is the ability to create relationships with prospective clients or strategic partners. How is this done? In marketing, you need to become visible as an expert, or partner with others who have entry into your desired markets. In selling, you need to develop the trust and confidence of your prospective client."

Tes Welborn, Ed.D., management consultant
and business coach, Teresa Welborn and Associates

olutions, you have probably experienced the following scenario. You make new commitments when you are feeling enthusiastic, reenergized, or just plain fed up with the way things are. But then something stops you from following through.

What is that something? Lack of time—and its frequent companion, not enough money—are easy excuses, but the fact is that most of us make choices about where to spend our time and money every day. We choose whether to make a cold call or chat with a friend; pay the admission price to a networking event or buy a movie ticket. And it's not just choosing between work and play. Suddenly that growing stack of junk mail may seem more important than writing a marketing letter, or buying a cell phone becomes more urgent than paying the cost of updating your portfolio.

If you are really serious about making this time different, about following through on your commitments and getting the results you want, it's time to look at what will get in the way. Are you worried or afraid? Of what? Are you resisting something? What is it? Is there some special permission that you need in order to be successful with this program?

Many people, perhaps most people, are routinely blocked in marketing and sales by self-sabotaging thinking or behavior. If you thought you were the only one suffering from terminal procrastination or struggling with negative messages from your own inner critic, know that you are not alone. Giving yourself permission to alter a long-standing habit can be a powerful step in the direction of lasting change. In the Get Clients Now! program, you will be consciously granting yourself a special permission every day. Here are some examples:

> *I have permission to ask for what I want.*
>
> *I am able to do what I'm afraid of.*
>
> *I deserve to be successful.*
>
> *I can make a good living and still have time for fun.*

The best way to design a special permission is to ask yourself what it is that you routinely think or do that prevents you from being successful at marketing. For example, suppose you never seem to have time to make follow-up calls because you are busy working on client projects. You know this behavior backfires in the long run, because when you complete a project, there isn't another one waiting for you. The permission you might design for yourself is, "It's okay not to do the clients' work first."

Or suppose that you are stalling in completing your portfolio, because then you will actually have to show it to someone. And if you did that, she might not like your work. Of course, you also know that if you don't show your portfolio to anyone, it's unlikely that anyone will hire you. In this case, you might choose this special permission: "I believe in my talents and abilities."

Are you wondering what is going to make you believe your special permission? After all, you just made it up. What will make it real for you? For one thing, there is the simple repetition of it. Repetition is one of the primary ways that we learn. You learned the alphabet by heart from saying or singing it over and over. If you look in the mirror each morning and say, "I believe in my talents and abilities," you will begin to internalize that information in the same way that you know "F" comes before "G" without reciting the alphabet from the beginning.

The other reason the special permission will work is that it's only for 28 days. Whenever you find yourself questioning the validity of your permission, remind yourself it is only temporary. You can go back to your old way of operating at the end of the month (if you still want to). Just as what dramatists call

"I joined a Get Clients Now!–oriented group three years ago when I needed to expand my business. In my false sense of courage, I didn't even know I had fear at first, but I felt stuck. During the program, I recognized that I needed to give myself permission to be afraid. I came up with a metaphor that would help me visualize it: 'Be the bunny.' On the Native American medicine wheel, the rabbit represents fear, and working with Rabbit Medicine requires owning your fear when you have it.

"I imagined myself as a rabbit hopping through fear—timid-but-still-moving bunny—or a rabbit in a World War I fighter plane with goggles and ears flopping in the wind—fearless bunny. It made being fearful seem funny, safe, and okay enough that I could deal with the task at hand. It really got me unstuck."

Shannon Seek, Certified Professional and Personal Coach, Seek Solutions, www.SeekSolutions.com

the "willing suspension of disbelief" can be the key to enjoying a movie or play, you can allow yourself to believe fully in your special permission temporarily. If you are skeptical, try it.

If you have a special permission, write it on the last line of your action worksheet. If you're still having trouble finding a permission that fits, just pick one to start with. It's almost a guarantee that some block or obstacle will appear within the first few days of starting the program. Then you can design a new special permission to address it. And if at any point during the 28 days, your permission stops working for you, change it.

# Chapter 6

# You're Ready ... Let's Go!
# Putting the System Into Action

*Whatever you can do, or dream you can, begin it.*
*Boldness has genius, power, and magic in it.*

—Goethe

Your action worksheet is completed—you have chosen your program goal, 1 to 3 success ingredients, 10 daily actions, and your special permission. It's time to put your own personal Get Clients Now! program into action!

## The Tracking Worksheet

The primary tool for the 28 days of the Get Clients Now! program is the tracking worksheet, which you will use to track your progress through the program every day. Using the tracking worksheet consistently will automatically provide you with the first four of the seven keys to achievement:

1. Focus

2. Evidence

3. Direction

4. Motivation

If you also arrange to work through the program with a buddy, group, or coach, you will lock in place the final three keys:

5. Accountability

6. Perspective

7. Support

Look at the partially completed tracking worksheet in Figure 6-1. Each column represents a working day of the program, for which you will make daily entries like this.

## Worksheet Categories

*Weather Report.* On a 1 to 10 scale, with 1 the lowest and 10 the highest, how are you today? How is your body? This is an intuitive score; put down whatever you feel is right. These numbers will go up and down from day to day, as your mood and physical condition fluctuate. This score tells you how much you should expect from yourself on any given day.

*Success Ingredients.* For each of your 1 to 3 success ingredient projects, what percentage have you completed? If 0 percent means you have done nothing yet and 100 percent means the project is done, how far do you estimate that have you progressed along the range? This may be an intuitive score, or for some projects you can compute it mathematically. These numbers will go up as projects move forward, but will not go down.

*Daily Actions.* For each of your 10 actions, did you do it today (Y) or not (N)? At the bottom of this section is a place to write the total number of actions completed at the end of each day. This number will go up and down from day to day, as your productivity varies and other activities require your attention. When an action is weekly (or several times per week) rather than daily, the score you give yourself each day depends on how well you carry out your plans. For example, if you plan to do something on Monday and you do it, you get a Y. If you planned it and didn't do it, you get an N. For any days you don't plan to do a particular weekly action, give yourself a free Y on that line. But if you get to the end of the week and still haven't done that thing, you must give yourself an N on Friday. Be honest. Remember, these scores are for you.

*Program Goal.* What percentage of your goal have you achieved so far? Since all goals in the program must be numerical, you should be able to compute this exactly. This number will go up as goals move forward, but will not go down.

*Special Permission.* Do you have your special permission today or not? Tell the truth. You will notice how hard everything is on the days when you don't have it.

On Day 1 of the program, you will start filling in your own tracking worksheet, based on the action worksheet you completed at the end of Chapter 5.

**Figure 6-1.** Partially completed tracking worksheet.

Start Date 9/11/99          GET CLIENTS NOW!™ Tracking Worksheet          Name

| | 9/13 | 9/14 | 9/15 | 9/16 | 9/17 | 9/20 | 9/21 | 9/22 | 9/23 | 9/24 | 9/27 | 9/28 | 9/29 | 9/30 | 10/1 | 10/4 | 10/5 | 10/6 | 10/7 | 10/8 |
|---|---|---|---|---|---|---|---|---|---|---|---|---|---|---|---|---|---|---|---|---|
| **Weather Report (1–10 scale)** | | | | | | | | | | | | | | | | | | | | |
| Me | 8 | 7 | 8 | 9 | 8 | | | | | | | | | | | | | | | |
| My Body | 7 | 7 | 8 | 8 | 7 | | | | | | | | | | | | | | | |
| **Success Ingredients (% done)** | | | | | | | | | | | | | | | | | | | | |
| 1  target mkt definition – 9/17 | 50 | 50 | 75 | 75 | 100 | | | | | | | | | | | | | | | |
| 2  10-second intro – 9/24 | 25 | 25 | 25 | 25 | 50 | | | | | | | | | | | | | | | |
| 3  8 networking venues – 10/1 | 0 | 0 | 13 | 25 | 25 | | | | | | | | | | | | | | | |
| **Daily Actions (Y/N)** | | | | | | | | | | | | | | | | | | | | |
| 1  1/2 hr/day on S.I.'s | N | N | Y | Y | Y | | | | | | | | | | | | | | | |
| 2  intro to group once/wk | Y | Y | Y | Y | Y | | | | | | | | | | | | | | | |
| 3  meet 20 new people/wk | Y | Y | Y | Y | N | | | | | | | | | | | | | | | |
| 4  2 networking events/wk | Y | Y | Y | Y | Y | | | | | | | | | | | | | | | |
| 5  lunch w/colleague wkly | Y | Y | Y | Y | Y | | | | | | | | | | | | | | | |
| 6  call 1 new person/day | N | Y | N | Y | Y | | | | | | | | | | | | | | | |
| 7  1 referral partner/wk | Y | Y | Y | Y | Y | | | | | | | | | | | | | | | |
| 8  info to 3 clients/wk | N | Y | N | Y | Y | | | | | | | | | | | | | | | |
| 9  ask for referral/day | Y | Y | N | Y | N | | | | | | | | | | | | | | | |
| 10  visualize success daily | Y | Y | Y | Y | Y | | | | | | | | | | | | | | | |
| Total (# of 10) | 7 | 9 | 7 | 10 | 8 | | | | | | | | | | | | | | | |
| **Program Goal (% of target)** 4 new clients | 0 | 0 | 0 | 0 | 25 | | | | | | | | | | | | | | | |
| **Special Permission? (Y/N)** enough time for everything | Y | Y | N | Y | Y | | | | | | | | | | | | | | | |

"Coaching works for many reasons that overlap and entwine, but one of the strongest threads in this weave is accountability. It is often the accountability alone that draws people to coaching. They may be competent and successful in many phases of their lives, but there is one area where they have found they cannot make the changes they want to make alone. They're just not getting it done, and they want the structure of a partnership to help them do the thing that is hard to do.

"How many times in your life have you said you were going to do something, and then not done it because nobody else would know the difference? Just the simple act of telling your plan to another person raises the stakes. On a freezing January morning, you might be tempted to pull the covers back over your head rather than go to the health club alone. But if you've promised to meet someone there at seven o'clock, there is a much better chance you'll actually get your chilly butt out of bed and go."

Laura Whitworth, Certified
Professional and Personal Coach,
Coaches Training Institute,
www.TheCoaches.com

## The 28-Day Program

For the next 28 days, you will be working steadily on achieving your chosen marketing goal. But if you keep your foot on the accelerator the whole time, you will run out of gas!

For that reason, there are rest days built into the program so you can have time to regroup and recharge. You may occasionally choose to spend some of a rest day working on a success ingredient project, but you are responsible for completing your daily actions only five days per week. In the program outline that follows, your rest days are assumed to be back to back, on Saturday and Sunday. If your workweek is different, you will need to adjust the program days to fit your real schedule.

**Figure 6-2.** Tracking worksheet.

GET CLIENTS NOW!™ Tracking Worksheet

Start Date _____                                                                Name _____

| | | | | | | | | | | | | | | | | | | | | | | | | | | |
|---|---|---|---|---|---|---|---|---|---|---|---|---|---|---|---|---|---|---|---|---|---|---|---|---|---|---|---|
| **Weather Report** (1–10 scale) | | | | | | | | | | | | | | | | | | | | | | | | | | | |
| Me | | | | | | | | | | | | | | | | | | | | | | | | | | | |
| My Body | | | | | | | | | | | | | | | | | | | | | | | | | | | |
| **Success Ingredients** (% done) | | | | | | | | | | | | | | | | | | | | | | | | | | | |
| 1 | | | | | | | | | | | | | | | | | | | | | | | | | | | |
| 2 | | | | | | | | | | | | | | | | | | | | | | | | | | | |
| 3 | | | | | | | | | | | | | | | | | | | | | | | | | | | |
| **Daily Actions** (Y/N) | | | | | | | | | | | | | | | | | | | | | | | | | | | |
| 1 | | | | | | | | | | | | | | | | | | | | | | | | | | | |
| 2 | | | | | | | | | | | | | | | | | | | | | | | | | | | |
| 3 | | | | | | | | | | | | | | | | | | | | | | | | | | | |
| 4 | | | | | | | | | | | | | | | | | | | | | | | | | | | |
| 5 | | | | | | | | | | | | | | | | | | | | | | | | | | | |
| 6 | | | | | | | | | | | | | | | | | | | | | | | | | | | |
| 7 | | | | | | | | | | | | | | | | | | | | | | | | | | | |
| 8 | | | | | | | | | | | | | | | | | | | | | | | | | | | |
| 9 | | | | | | | | | | | | | | | | | | | | | | | | | | | |
| 10 | | | | | | | | | | | | | | | | | | | | | | | | | | | |
| **Total** (# of 10) | | | | | | | | | | | | | | | | | | | | | | | | | | | |
| **Program Goal** (% of target) | | | | | | | | | | | | | | | | | | | | | | | | | | | |
| **Special Permission?** (Y/N) | | | | | | | | | | | | | | | | | | | | | | | | | | | |

**Day 1**

Saturday is a great day to begin your program. Close the door, turn off the phone, and bring out your completed action worksheet from Chapter 5. Make an enlarged copy of the blank tracking worksheet in Figure 6-2 (on the preceding page), and fill in the dates on the top line and the information in Column 1. See Figure 6-1 for an example.

On the top line, write the calendar dates of your working days for the next month. If today were Saturday, September 11, for example, you would label the first 10 columns on your worksheet 9/13–9/17, and 9/20–9/24, skipping the Saturday and Sunday rest days in between. Next, write in Column 1 the success ingredients from your action worksheet, with the target dates you chose for each one. Then, add your 10 daily actions, program goal, and special permission.

Award yourself a starting score on each of your success ingredients and your program goal. Are you starting from zero on your success ingredient projects and the goal you set for the month, or have you already made some progress? The worksheet in Figure 6-1 shows a starting score of 50 percent on target market definition, because the person filling it out believed he was already halfway there. On his "10-second introduction," he had done some work but needed more, so he scored himself at 25 percent. For "networking venues," he had done nothing yet, so he started at zero.

To give yourself an accurate score, you may need to quantify your success ingredient projects. For success ingredients like networking venues or referral partners, ask yourself, "How many is enough?" If you're not sure, look at the appropriate chapter in Part III for more guidance. Write the number you choose on your worksheet as for networking venues in the example. If you have chosen a more intangible success ingredient such as networking skills or telemarketing skills, score yourself intuitively. If zero equals "phone phobic" and 100 percent means "expert telemarketer," where would you rate yourself today? Would you like to be at 100 percent at the end of the program, or would 50 percent satisfy you? If it's the latter, write down "telemarketing skills at 50 percent," so you know what you're aiming for.

Now award yourself a starting score on your program goal. As described in Chapter 3, this is a numerical target for clients, contracts, appointments, billable hours, total revenue, or new prospects. You may be starting at zero, or you may have made some progress already. Either way, be honest with yourself, and be specific about what you are counting. Is a new client anyone who schedules his first appointment, or does this count only after the person shows up for it? Is your total revenue what you bill this month, or what you actually collect? Base your score on a way of measuring that will make this goal truly meaningful for you.

Now put the tracking worksheet where you will be sure to see it first thing on Monday morning. Are you ready to make a commitment to the program you have designed for yourself?

**Thought for the day:** Jay Conrad Levinson, author of the Guerrilla Marketing series, often says the following when asked about his work: "I hate to admit this, but mediocre marketing with commitment works better than brilliant marketing without commitment."

**Day 2**

**Rest Day.** Do something you really enjoy, perhaps an activity you haven't had time for in a while. You're going to be working hard for the next month, so take this opportunity to have some fun. Get plenty of sleep tonight, so you'll be fresh and ready to go in the morning.

**Thought for the day:** Even God rested one day a week.

**Day 3**

Are you ready to get clients now? It's time to let the tracking worksheet start doing its magic. As soon as you sit down at your desk this morning, put your tracking worksheet in front of you. Each working day of the program, you will be using the worksheet at least twice: once at the beginning of the day and once at the end. To let even more of the worksheet's magic rub off on you, post it where you can't miss seeing it all day long.

On this first Monday, begin by doing your first **Morning Review**. Look over your success ingredients and daily actions. Which of these tasks do you plan to work on today? Do you need to add them to your daily to-do list? Check your special permission, to remind yourself what you need to be successful. Okay, you're ready for the day. Go for it!

At day's end, award yourself your first **Daily Scores:**

*Weather Report:* You and your body on a scale of 1–10.
Success Ingredients: The status of each project from 0–100 percent complete.
*Daily Actions:* Y for yes and N for no on each one. Add up the total number of Y's at the bottom.
*Program Goal:* Progress toward your goal from 0–100 percent accomplished.
*Special Permission:* Y if you have it today and N if you don't.

If you have questions on how to score yourself, refer to the description of the tracking worksheet at the beginning of this chapter.

You made it through your first working day of the Get Clients Now! program. Did you get everything done you wanted to? If you did, great! If not, look at your list again tomorrow to see if you need to make changes. Throughout the rest of the program, the day-by-day guidelines here will focus on keeping you in action, on track, and motivated. Whenever you have questions about how to implement the daily actions or success ingredients you chose, refer to the appropriate chapter in Part III for detailed logistical help.

**Thought for the day:** A short poem about marketing:

> You have to sow a lot of seeds.
> Some are flowers; some are weeds;
> Some will die while others grow,
> But all depends on how many you sow.

**Day 4**

Begin the day with your **Morning Review**. Look at your success ingredients, daily actions, and special permission, and plan how you will include them in the day's agenda. You will do this each working day of the program. In today's review, and for all of this first week, pay special attention to the daily actions you chose. How did it work for you to add these new activities into your day?

If you scored an 8 or above on your daily actions yesterday, keep them as they are. If you scored lower, but yesterday was unusually busy or chaotic, give yourself another day to see how you do. But if you're feeling overwhelmed and suspect that your choices may have been too ambitious, you have complete permission to scale back a bit. Rather than eliminating any of the actions you chose, try reducing the level of effort. Is there something you committed to do daily that could happen three times per week instead? Or could you cut down on the number of calls, letters, or meetings you had planned? Now is the time to redesign a list of actions that will work for you within the reality of a normal day.

At the end of the day, do your **Daily Scores**. Did you do better today? Terrific! Still not happy with your scores? Don't worry. You will continue to look at ways of making them improve.

**Thought for the day:** You will never be completely ready. Start from wherever you are.

**Day 5**

**Morning Review**. Wednesday is the day to look at any actions scheduled as weekly that haven't happened yet. Choose right now which day you will do them. If a lunch or meeting is involved, place a call to make the appointment or reservation that will lock it in.

**Daily Scores**. Have you reached a score of 8 or more on your daily actions yet? If so, good work! Try setting up a reward for yourself if you reach a certain score tomorrow. If today was a 6, go for an 8; if today was a 9, make tomorrow a 10.

**Thought for the day:** Everyone you meet is either a potential client or a source of referrals. Never pass up an opportunity to introduce yourself.

**Day 6**

**Morning Review.** What will be your reward if you reach your target for daily actions today? What do you need to do to make that score possible? Here are three strategies to try:

1. *Do it first.* Don't allow yourself to do anything else until your daily actions are completed. Don't pick up your messages, look at the mail, or answer the phone. Eliminate every possible distraction until you have reached your target score for today.

2. *Do it now.* You may have some daily actions that can't be done first because they need to occur in the course of the business day. Every time you think of one of them, do it immediately. Let's say you need to ask for one referral per day. When you are in conversation with someone, as soon as you think of it, just ask for a referral— right then, no matter what you are talking about. If you find yourself forgetting, put a rubber band around your wrist, and let it remind you each time you notice it.

3. *Block out time.* If your schedule won't permit doing all your daily actions first, block out some time on your calendar. Make a specific appointment with yourself, and honor it just as if someone else was expecting you. Use this appointment as an excuse if other people try to detain you. If you're afraid you'll forget or get busy with something else, set an alarm.

**Daily Scores.** Did you earn your reward today? Congratulations! If you're still having trouble, review your daily actions list again. If you find it too ambitious, you can scale back your level of effort at any point during the program, as long as you stick to the guidelines for choosing daily actions given in Chapter 5. You may decide that you already have the right list, but the problem you need to solve is how to make it happen. Try using the three strategies listed above again tomorrow. It may take you several tries to change your work habits so that marketing becomes a part of your day. Keep at it; the payoff will be worth the effort.

**Thought for the day:** Learning any new habit is like starting an exercise program: It can be painful at first, but as you exercise that particular muscle, it becomes stronger and supports you better. Over time, the pain gives way to tolerance, tolerance to satisfaction, and satisfaction to exhilaration as you see the results of your commitment and persistence.

**Day 7**

**Morning Review**. It's your last chance to complete any actions scheduled as weekly, so look now at how to fit them in. What daily actions score will you go for today?

**Daily Scores**. How did you do this week? If you got your daily actions score up to 8 or more, celebrate your achievement. You are on the path to success in getting more clients and reaching your program goal. If your scores are in the 5 to 7 range, you are getting close, but need to make some changes. Revisit the morning review for Days 4 and 6 to see what else you might do. If you are consistently scoring lower than 5 on daily actions, you are not failing; you are learning. There is something in your way, and once you know what it is, you can begin to eliminate it. We'll look at some of these potential roadblocks tomorrow.

Complete your week by making a list of your wins over the last seven days. What worked? What went right? What great things did you do, say, receive, and achieve? Put your "wins list" where you can see it, right next to your tracking worksheet. Then congratulate yourself; you stuck with the program through Week 1.

**Thought for the day:** There are benefits of doing business with you that you take for granted but that would astonish your clients and prospects if they knew about them. Look for the hidden assets in your business, and be sure to reveal them in your marketing.

## Day 8

**Rest Day**. In the first week of the program, you may have encountered two of the biggest obstacles to marketing success: fear and resistance. If looking at some of the items on your daily actions list made your stomach flutter or your throat get tight, that was fear. If you found yourself thinking, "I don't wanna!" and digging in your heels, that was resistance. Know that you are not alone in these feelings. You may not hear other folks talk about this at the Chamber of Commerce, but most people in business feel afraid, resistant, or both, about certain elements of marketing.

Finding out where those feelings came from and why you have them is beyond the scope of this book. What you need right now is to get past them in order to be successful. The first step in removing these roadblocks is to recognize that they are there, and get very specific about their nature. Answer these questions right now:

1. *What are you afraid of?* Being rejected? Making a mistake? Failing? Succeeding? Looking silly? Write down as many different fears as you can think of. If you feel stuck, ask yourself, "What do I think would happen if I..." and complete the sentence with whatever daily actions are giving you trouble—perhaps "...introduced myself in front of a group" or "...made a cold call."

2. *What are you resisting?* Having to do the work? Bragging about yourself? Spending time on marketing when you have other urgent priorities? Finish this sentence in your best whining voice, "I don't wanna..."

Now that these barriers are out in the open, ask yourself if you are going to let them stop you. They don't have to. You can feel afraid yet move forward; you can feel resistant yet still do what you are resisting. The next time you are having trouble, notice what you are feeling, and choose whether to let it keep you from taking action. Say to yourself, "Oh, there's the fear again," or "Wow, I'm really feeling resistant right now," and keep going.

**Thought for the day:** Having courage doesn't mean that you are fearless. It means you can feel the fear and take action anyway.

**Day 9**

**Rest Day**. Reward yourself for a week well done. Spend an entire day not thinking about work. Do something relaxing and replenishing.

**Thought for the day:** You are the biggest asset your business has. Taking care of yourself is taking care of business.

**Day 10**

**Morning Review**. Continue planning your day to include all your daily actions, and try for a score of 8 or higher daily. In this second week, we will shift the focus to your success ingredient projects. How has your progress been here? You are one-fourth of the way through the program, so you should be 25 percent ahead of where you started on your success ingredients. If you are working on three at the same time, you should have moved them all along that far. If you are doing them one after the other, you should be almost done with the first.

**Daily Scores**. Were you able to give your success ingredients enough attention today? Look now at the rest of the week, and see where you can fit them in. By Friday, you should be halfway through in order to stay on track.

**Thought for the day:** Work expands to fill the time allotted to it. If you want to get more done, give each task only the amount of time it is worth to you. And if you want to work less, allow less time for work.

**Day 11**

**Morning Review.** Are you having trouble finding enough time for your success ingredients? If you are on or ahead of schedule, good for you! If not, here are some strategies to help:

1. *Give something away.* What else is on your to-do list right now? Is there anything there you can hand off to someone else? If you can't unload an entire project, are there some pieces you could ask another person to do? If you are unaccustomed to delegating, you may need to expand your vision of what it looks like. You don't need an administrative assistant in order to delegate; you can delegate to a co-worker, a colleague, a friend, your spouse, your children, your siblings, another committee member, or a paid professional. What are you doing that doesn't need you to do it? Can you ask someone else? Can you pay someone else? If it enabled you to spend an extra hour a day on marketing, could you afford to pay someone to handle some of your responsibilities?

2. *Put something off.* What on your list really doesn't have to be done right now? If you have a habit of planning more things than you can possibly do, you are already putting some things off by default. Why not choose up front what those things will be? Think in terms of your overall priorities. What is more important than marketing? There will certainly be a few things, such as servicing your current clients or spending some time with your family, but it's unlikely that everything on your list is more important than marketing right now. Find some tasks that you can defer for the next 17 days.

3. *Let something go.* If you have had a task on your list for three weeks or more and not gotten it done, does it need to be done at all? If you haven't made time for it in that long, how important can it be? Try this: cross it off the list for one week, and see if it comes back to haunt you. If you can forget about it, that's one less thing to do. If you can't let it drop, look at options 1 and 2 again.

**Daily Scores**. Did you make more headway on success ingredients today? What will be your target scores for tomorrow?

**Thought for the day:** Positioning expert Jack Trout says that the average American is exposed to 200,000 marketing messages per year. Remember that when you're wondering if it's too soon to follow up with someone who has heard from you before.

## Day 12

**Morning Review**. You have three days left to hit the 50 percent mark on your success ingredients. What will it take? If you are having any logistical challenges or how-to questions, read the chapter in Part III about the marketing cycle stage you are working on.

**Daily Scores**. Did you hit your target scores? Take a moment to celebrate! Are you still struggling? You may need some additional support. Call your business buddy or a friend, and ask for help in the following very specific way:

1. *Set a fixed time to talk*. Whether you meet by phone or in person, set a starting and ending time for your conversation. This will tighten the focus on solving your problem. Half an hour is enough; an hour is plenty.

2. *Begin by clearing*. Ask your buddy to just listen while you tell him or her what's going on. Your buddy can say things like, "Gee, that's tough," or "How awful!" but should not offer any advice until you are through. Talk about not only what is happening, but how it makes you feel. If it sounds like complaining, that probably means you're doing it right. You might be saying something like this: "I've been trying for two weeks to finish my brochure, and there's just been one emergency after another, and now my mother wants me to help sell her car, and I'm so frustrated! All the words I write down just come out wrong, and I don't think it'll ever come together, and I needed it yesterday, and I'm so worried that..." You get the idea.

Set a time limit of 5 to 10 minutes for clearing. At the end of that time, ask your buddy to summarize for you: "I hear how frustrated and worried you are. You seem to have two problems that need to be solved: finding the time to work on the brochure, and getting the words to come out right. Are you ready to look at some solutions?"

3. *Brainstorm possible solutions.* Now that your problems are out in the open, you can get some assistance in solving them. Your buddy's job is not to hand you the right answer; it is to help you expand your thinking to come up with some new ideas. Take your problems one at time, and together with your buddy, make a list of possible solutions. Don't edit the list as you are brainstorming; you will do that later. Anything and everything that comes up should go on the list. You are not allowed to say, "That won't work" or "I already tried that." Here are the potential results of a brainstorm on getting the right words for a brochure:

   - Hire a copywriter.
   - Use the thesaurus.
   - Do a brochure with only pictures.
   - Look at the Yellow Pages.
   - Use what I have and stop worrying.
   - Plagiarize my competitors' literature.
   - Ask my cousin the writer to help.
   - Don't use a brochure at all.
   - Take a class in marketing communications.
   - Have some colleagues review it.

4. *Look for a next step.* You can ask your buddy to help you with this, or do it later on your own. If none of the brainstormed ideas seems right, look at each one to see if there's something useful in it. Maybe you can't afford a copywriter, but you know one you could ask for some free advice. Perhaps a class in marketing communications would take too long, but you could check out a textbook from the library. Find just one thing you can do that will get you moving forward again.

   **Thought for the day:** It really doesn't matter what you choose; the important thing is that you choose.

**Day 13**

**Morning Review.** Set a target for your success ingredient scores today that is a no-kidding-whatever-it-takes goal. Remember that you said you needed these things to be successful.

**Daily Scores.** Did you make it? Congratulations! Not quite there? You have one more day to catch up. Take a moment to remind yourself of your special permission. Did you have it today? If not, what do you need to do, say, or believe to grant yourself that permission? Now that you have been working with the program for a while, is there any another permission you have discovered that you need? It's okay to switch, or even have two of them if that serves you in moving forward.

**Thought for the day:** If some people don't say your price is too high, you're not charging enough.

**Day 14**

**Morning Review.** It's the halfway point in your Get Clients Now! program. Where do you want to be at the end of the day?

**Daily Scores.** You have worked really hard this week, so pat yourself on the back. If you achieved your target scores on daily actions and success ingredients, you are on your way to a successful conclusion at month's end. If you haven't been doing as well as you would like, look at how much more you have accomplished than in the two weeks before you started the program. If you haven't hit the 50 percent mark with your success ingredients, revisit the morning review for Day 11, or schedule another call with your buddy to see what else you might do.

Complete your week by making and posting your wins list. Hooray! You made it through Week 2!

**Thought for the day:** There is no failure, only feedback.

**Day 15**

**Rest Day.** During Week 2, it's a good bet that you found yourself having at least one conversation with your inner critic. Also known as the committee, negative self-talk, or the gremlin, this is the voice in your head that makes comments like these: "You're not good enough," "You don't know how," and "They won't like me." The inner critic tends to have a lot to say about sales and marketing. This is a place in your life where you are putting yourself on the line, and it brings up all of your concerns about being inadequate. Negative self-talk is one of the biggest obstacles you must overcome to achieve success.

Everyone has an inner critic, but some people manage it better than others. It is even possible to manage it so well that you hardly notice it. To begin managing your inner critic, here are some steps to follow:

1. *Raise your awareness.* Every time you find yourself fearful, nervous, hesitant, or second-guessing, stop and ask what is going on in your head. You may have a particular behavior pattern that shows up when the inner critic is active, such as procrastinating, avoiding people or tasks, or starting and stopping activities. Or there may be a body sensation you can use as a warning sign, like a tight throat, sweaty palms, or a sinking feeling in your stomach. When you notice any of these signs of negative self-talk, pause to listen to the conversation. Write down what your inner critic says to you, and keep a list.

2. *Take responsibility.* Once you have a catalog of your inner critic's greatest hits, recognize that you can choose to change the music. Just as with fear and resistance, you don't have to let these nega-

tive messages stop you. Begin by constructing a fair and accurate response to each of the messages you typically hear, and use your response whenever you notice it. If your gremlin is saying, "You should be working," you might respond, "I've worked hard this week and deserve a day off." If the inner critic tells you, "Don't do that—you might make a mistake," a good answer is, "Yes, I might, but I'll learn from it and move on." Learning to manage negative self-talk is a skill that you can learn. The only requirement is that you be willing to try.

3. *Practice self-management.* Learning any new skill takes practice, and managing your inner critic is no different. In the beginning, it may be difficult to catch your inner critic in the act; you may realize only later where the reluctance you were feeling came from. This is a normal part of learning self-management. Just use your positive response as soon as you think of it. With practice, you will become more skilled at hearing negative messages in "real time," and be able to respond to them immediately. If you use this process consistently, the messages will begin to lose their power over you, because you will stop believing them.

**Thought for the day:** The main difference between a skill and a talent is a lot of practice.

**Day 16**

Rest Day. Have fun today! Enjoy an activity you haven't done for a while, so the day feels special. You deserve it!

**Thought for the day:** Rule One in the game of life: You must be present to win.

**Day 17**

**Morning Review.** It's the first working day of Week 3, and you're past the halfway mark in the program. Your target scores for each day this week should continue to be 8 or higher on your daily actions, and 50 to 75 percent on your success ingredients. The focus this week will be on your program goal. At this point in the program, you should have reached at least 50 percent of your goal. By the week's end, you will need to be at 75 percent. Ask yourself this morning, "What will it take to make that happen?"

**Daily Scores.** Did you see some movement toward your program goal today? If you are already at 75 percent or above, consider raising the stakes. How much more business could you generate by the end of next week? If you're below 50 percent, look at your daily actions once more. Do you need to boost your level of effort in order to get clients? Consider increasing the quantity or frequency of your daily actions to make up the gap between you and your goal. Make your weekly actions twice a week; double your target number for calls, letters, or meetings. You've got only two weeks left, so make the most of them.

**Thought for the day:**

> If he who has a thing to sell
> Goes and whispers in a well,
> He won't be so apt to make the dollars
> As he who climbs a tree and hollers!
>
> —Anonymous

**Day 18**

**Morning Review.** What can you do that will allow your program goal to pull you toward it, instead of having to push to get there? Take a moment to reread the first section of your action worksheet from Chapter 3. How did you answer the question, "What would that get you?" when you thought about the level of business you really want? Visualize some of those results right now. Pick one of them to be your touchstone for the day, and post a word, phrase, or picture to represent it on your phone or computer.

**Daily Scores.** Did you feel some pull from your goal today? Try creating an even stronger touchstone for yourself this evening with one of these quick activities:

1. *Write about it.* Write down what it would be like to achieve your goal. What would you have? How would you feel? What could you then do?

2. *Draw it.* Draw a picture of what goal achievement would look like. You don't have to be an artist; stick figures drawn with markers will do the trick.

3. *Visualize it.* Close your eyes, put on some soothing music, and create a detailed vision of success in your mind's eye.

4. *Sing it.* If there's a song that represents achievement or good fortune to you, play it and sing along. Or change the words to any song on the radio to be about you and your success.

**Thought for the day:** When doing business with the universe, remember that you must place an order if you want to get a delivery.

**Day 19**

**Morning Review.** Use the touchstone you created yesterday to help motivate you today. Post your essay or picture on the wall, recapture your visualization by briefly closing your eyes, or hum your success song.

**Daily Scores.** Are you past the 50 percent mark toward your program goal? Yes? Keep it up! No? If you are still struggling, revisit the place in Chapter 2 where you chose which stage of the universal marketing cycle you would work on this month. Has anything changed or shifted since you made your choice? If you're not sure, look at the daily actions listed in Chapter 5 for the other stage or stages you are considering. Do any of those actions seem more appropriate for where you are now?

If you've been working at a high level of activity for the last two and a half weeks, it is entirely possible that you have moved forward a stage in the marketing cycle. It's also possible that by becoming more active about marketing, you have discovered that your challenges are not what you originally thought they were. If either of these situations exists for you, it's time to redo your daily actions list to match better where you are now.

**Thought for the day:** When you are selling professional services, the customer's resistance is often about taking the action that your service represents, and not at all about hiring you. If you can get the customer to commit to taking action on what needs to be done, hiring you will be his natural next step.

**Day 20**

**Morning Review.** You have two days left to reach a 75 percent score on your program goal. What sort of game could you design for yourself to play that would make these two days exciting and fun? Could you see how many phone calls you could make in an hour, or how many business cards you could collect at one meeting? Is there a buddy you could play this game with, and have the winner buy lunch?

**Daily Scores.** What was it like to be more playful with marketing today? Could you play the same game tomorrow or invent another? What could you reward yourself with this weekend if you get to 75 percent on your program goal by the end of Friday?

**Thought for the day:** Struggle and adventure are two sides of the same coin. When you find yourself struggling, flip it over.

**Day 21**

**Morning Review.** Set yourself up for an exciting, adventurous day. Take some risks, put yourself out there, and really go for it.

**Daily Scores.** It's the end of Week 3, and you have been steadily in action about marketing for 21 days. You definitely deserve some applause. If you are at 75 percent or higher on your program goal, you are right on target. If you aren't quite there, congratulate yourself anyway because you are learning a great deal. We'll look tomorrow at whether you need to make any changes.

**Thought for the day:** Marketing is like a box of chocolates because: (1) You never know what you're going to get; (2) nobody likes all of it; and (3) there are plenty of treats, but you have to look to find them.

**Day 22**

**Rest Day.** Does it look as if you'll be able to reach 100 percent of your goal by the end of next week? It's time to revisit your goal one more time and see if it is serving you the way it should. Goals work differently for different people. Some folks like ambitious goals that they can't quite reach, because it makes them try harder. Others find that this approach backfires, because they always feel as if they're not doing enough. Setting a goal that they know they can achieve is much more satisfying. Which of these types are you?

If ambitious goals excite you and make you want to get up in the morning, and your program goal is at 75 percent or more right now, raise it. Give yourself a reason to go all out in the final week. If, on the other hand, it's important to you that you reach every goal you set for yourself and you're below 75 percent right now, lower your target. This is not cheating! If you can't win the game, there will be a piece of you that doesn't want to play any more. By setting a more achievable goal, you will continue to be motivated by it.

**Thought for the day:** Goal setting works the same way as target practice. Without a target, you don't know what you're shooting at, and until you start shooting, you don't know how far off your aim is.

### Day 23

**Rest Day.** Did you promise yourself a reward for reaching your program goal target this week? Today is the day to keep your promise. If you didn't make your target, what reward do you get for trying?

**Thought for the day:** Rest restores, repose repositions, recreation re-creates.

**Day 24**

**Morning Review.** You're on the home stretch, with only five more days to go. Your target scores for each day this week should be 8 or higher on your daily actions, and 75 to 100 percent on your success ingredients and your program goal. Picture the reward for achieving your program goal that you chose in Chapter 3. If you reach your goal by Friday, the prize will be yours.

The focus of Week 4 is on learning. As you have been working your way through this program, you have discovered some significant information about how you handle marketing. If you can capture that learning and use it to become a better marketer, you will have accomplished an important result this month. Finding out that you never leave enough time for follow-up is just as valuable to your ultimate success as getting three new clients. As you plan your day this morning and complete your daily actions throughout the day, notice what you have learned about time management. Are you managing projects, priorities, and your schedule any differently than you did at the beginning of the month? What is working for you about the way you manage time? What isn't?

**Daily Scores.** Were you able to balance all the program elements today: success ingredients, daily actions, program goal, and special permission? Take a few moments to write down your learning about time management over the past 24 days.

**Thought for the day:**

> There once was a person named Lou
> Who found he had too much to do.
> So his very first task
> Was learning to ask
> Who to give Lou's to-dos to?

## Day 25

**Morning Review.** Have you designed a getting-clients game to play this week, or is there some other way you can keep marketing light and fun? Humor and a sense of playfulness are effective antidotes to fear and resistance. Notice throughout today what you are learning about these two tough adversaries.

### Daily Scores

- What have you learned about fear and resistance?
- When do fear and resistance surface for you?
- What does their appearance signal?
- What strategies have worked for you in handling these saboteurs?
- Where do you still have trouble?

**Thought for the day:** When you are faced with an obstacle, imagine you are an inquisitive child at a locked gate. Depending on your skills and talents, you might climb over it, tunnel under it, go for help, pick the lock, or break down the fence. The one thing you wouldn't do is stand there wondering how it got locked in the first place.

**Day 26**

**Morning Review.** Keep that reward visible; you're almost there! If you have been using a business buddy, action group, or coach, is there any extra assistance you'd like to ask for in these last three days to help you over the top? Consider today what you have learned about support this month.

**Daily Scores.** As of today, your program goal should be at 90 percent or more. Ask yourself what you should do in the next two days to reach 100 percent. Focus especially on support—for example:

- Is there any support you need to ask for from your family, friends, or colleagues?
- What kind of support has been most helpful to you in the past month?
- Have you found yourself willing to ask for support, or do you wait until you are in a crisis?
- What support structures would be beneficial to maintain after you complete the program?

**Thought for the day:** Asking for help is not cheating. It's how anything important ever gets done.

**Day 27**

**Morning Review.** Is there anything that will get in the way of your being successful today? Are you willing to set aside whatever comes up? Notice what you are learning about self-management.

**Daily Scores.** Only one more day to go. Take a deep breath, and smile a big smile. Now focus on your inner critic:

- Have you gotten better acquainted with your inner critic during the program?
- What are the "greatest hits" playing on your negative self-talk jukebox?
- Are there some countermessages you designed that work particularly well?
- How does your inner critic interfere with your ability to market?
- What changes have you noticed in your ability to manage this interference?

**Thought for the day:** If you don't like the music, don't dance to it.

**Day 28**

**Morning Review.** Are you ready to win? Are you planning your victory celebration? Can you taste your reward? You have earned it! Think about the element of motivation today:

- What really motivates you?
- How did having a specific goal for the month change your behavior?
- Does a far-off goal draw you toward it, or do you need to be getting more enjoyment in the moment?
- Do you reward yourself for progress and learning, or only if you achieve certain results?
- Are you satisfied with rewarding yourself, or do you want acknowledgment from others?
- What motivational techniques backfire on you? Which are your favorites?

**Daily Scores.** You did it! Congratulations! If you reached 100 percent or more on your program goal, you have achieved complete success in the Get Clients Now! program. If your score is lower, you still deserve a huge commendation for sticking with the program. And you probably learned even more than those who reached 100 percent.

What have you learned about goal setting, about marketing, about selling? What has been your learning if you didn't meet your goal? The fact is that marketing is just another skill that you learn by practicing over time, and you have had a lot of practice this month. If you tend to reward yourself only for results, try switching to acknowledging your progress, regardless of the outcome. You may find this shift in thinking beneficial in more areas than marketing.

**Thought for the day:** Success in marketing depends on success in management. The way you manage time, money, projects, people, and your own worst doubts and fears has as much to do with getting clients as advertising, publicity, and cold calling do. Always remember that what you are really selling is you, so developing yourself is the best marketing investment you can make.

## What's Next for You?

You've just completed an intensive 28-day program to get more clients. After you celebrate and catch your breath, you will probably be wondering what's next. The Get Clients Now! program is designed to be used over and over. Next month, or whenever else you feel the need for a marketing boost, you can design a new program for yourself and start again.

Whether or not you are ready to repeat the program right away, take a few moments to review your notes about what you learned. In each of the areas you examined in Week 4—time management, fear and resistance, support, self-management, and motivation—ask yourself what's next for you:

- How can you develop your skills in these areas to become better at marketing?

- What will you do differently in the future, based on what you learned throughout the program about goal setting, marketing, and selling?

Look also at your chosen success ingredients, and ask yourself:

- Are any of these projects still incomplete?

- What additional projects did you consider choosing back in Chapter 4?

- Is it time now to move forward on any of these others?

---

"One of the participants in a Get Clients Now!–oriented group we were leading described her experience this way: 'I'm good at what I do, but poor at marketing what I do. For ages I suffered in silence, ignorant of the power of a marketing plan and clear, directed, and persistent action. My business suffered and nearly died. With Get Clients Now! I gained a big-picture marketing perspective, and an "anyone-can-do-this-and-clearly-everyone-should" action plan (which created momentum).

"'I gained focus, clarity, and insight. Beyond the clear progress and definable results I received from participating, I also learned more about myself in 28 days than I would have imagined possible.'"

Sue Coleman, Certified Professional and Personal Coach, and Ricki Rush, Certified Professional and Personal Coach, LifeWorks!, www.lifeworks-coaching.com

Save your notes about learning areas and success ingredients to help design your next Get Clients Now! program. When you are ready to start again, begin by rediagnosing your marketing condition with the universal marketing cycle in Chapter 2.

If you went through the program by yourself this time, consider repeating it with a buddy, group, or coach, and see how much difference those extra three keys to achievement—accountability, perspective, and support—can make to your success. Or perhaps there is another way you see to make this program more effective for the way you think and work. Be creative, find your own unique solution, and, above all, have fun!

# Part III

# The Strategies

This part of the book contains marketing "recipes" to help you create your chosen success ingredients or employ the marketing strategies and tactics specified in your action plan. There is a chapter for each stage of the universal marketing cycle, so you need to look at only the chapter that covers the stage you are working on.

Each chapter begins with an overview of the stage, and then discusses how each marketing strategy used in it can be effectively employed. Only strategies suitable for the stage are included, usually in this order:

Direct Contact and Follow-Up

Networking and Referral Building

Public Speaking

Writing and Publicity

Promotional Events

Advertising

You need to study only those strategies you are actually planning to use. For each strategy, the appropriate tools (your success ingredients) are described along with the tactics (represented by your daily actions) that relate to them. For example, the success ingredient "prospect list" appears under the tactics "Calling and Mailing," and "press release or kit" under "Getting Media Publicity." The success ingredients described in each section are listed at the top so you can find them easily.

Happy cooking!

# Chapter 7

# Filling the Pipeline: When You Don't Have Enough Phone Numbers to Call

*Our grand business is not to see what lies dimly at a distance, but to do what lies clearly at hand.*

—Thomas Carlyle

### Making Your Strategies Work

Filling your marketing pipeline with prospects, contacts, leads, and referrals will be an ongoing process for as long as you are in business. By choosing to focus on this stage of the marketing cycle now, you are acknowledging that this is the area of your marketing that needs the most effort. Later, when you have overcome some of your pipeline-filling challenges, you may decide to focus more energy on one of the other stages. But it is important to recognize that you will always need to keep your pipeline full.

This means that whatever marketing strategies you decide on for filling the pipeline, you should be willing to keep them up over an extended period of time. In marketing, more of the same works much better than a little of everything. Ideally, your pipeline-filling activities should become automatic and habitual. Even when you are busy, you should always allow time for making new contacts, networking, speaking, or whatever your chosen strategies are.

It's natural to wonder whether the strategies you have selected are the best choices. You may find yourself wanting to switch around just to see if something else might work better. *Don't change your pipeline-filling strategies during the 28 days of the Get Clients Now! program*. It simply isn't enough time for you to judge your results accurately. It's okay to change *tactics*, say from cold calling to warm calling, but not overall *strategies*, from, say, networking and referral building to public speaking.

The only way to know how well a particular strategy is working to fill your pipeline is to track your results over time. There are three statistics that will be helpful to you in evaluating the strategies you are using:

1. How many prospects did each strategy generate?
2. How many sales resulted from those prospects?
3. What was the dollar value of those sales?

If you carefully note the exact source of each prospect, you can easily track these statistics for the month of the program. If you keep tracking your results for three months, six months, or a year, you will have a much more accurate picture of which strategies work the best. Then if you decide to make a change, choose one new strategy at a time to try out. And keep tracking.

## Who Belongs in Your Pipeline

There are two broad categories of people and organizations you want in your marketing pipeline: those who may someday be clients and those who can refer clients. To find people who are likely to become clients, reach out to a target market that is a good match for your service. To find people who may never be clients but could refer you business, reach out to those who serve or interact with that target market.

A person or group who doesn't fall into one of these two categories probably doesn't belong in your pipeline. It is true that people you meet in the course of doing business may become personal friends or helpful resources, but you don't want to use up your precious marketing time in following up with folks who are neither likely to be clients nor refer them.

Whenever you meet someone outside your target market who also doesn't seem to have much contact with it, think twice before putting that person in your pipeline. Always concentrate your efforts on the most likely prospects and referral partners. The way to win the marketing game is not to collect the most names and phone numbers, but to make the most sales.

## Global Pipeline-Filling Tools

*Success Ingredients*

description of services      10-second introduction

target market definition    business cards

## Description of Services

Being able to describe clearly the services you offer is essential for all aspects of marketing. Your service description can be the basis of numerous other marketing tools, such as a brochure or telephone script. A complete description contains the features, benefits, structure, and cost of your services. Here is an example for a certified public accountant serving small business owners:

> I provide tax preparation services for income, payroll, sales, and other miscellaneous taxes. I advise my clients on tax compliance and how to minimize their taxes. I also prepare business and personal financial statements. Other services I offer are analyzing employee benefit and retirement packages, valuing the worth of a business, and advice on accounting and financial software packages.
>
> Benefits of using my service include saving money on taxes, complying with government regulations to avoid penalties, having accurate information to manage your business at your fingertips, and letting someone else worry about keeping up with tax laws so you don't have to.
>
> I charge for my services on an hourly basis, at $100 per hour.

## Target Market Definition

Your target market is the prime audience for the service you are selling. It is the group of people or organizations you plan to pursue actively as clients. Don't make the mistake of thinking that your target market definition must encompass everyone who could be a client. Instead, decide whom you really want:

### How to Identify Your Target Market

- Who needs your service the most?
- Who is able to pay what you need to charge?
- Who is likely to give you large orders or repeat business?
- Whose problems and goals do you care about?
- Who would be the most fun and satisfying to work with?
- Where do you already have contacts?
- Who would be the easiest clients to get?

Remember that what you are doing here is targeting a particular group, not excluding all others. You are not limiting yourself by choosing a target market; you are organizing yourself to launch an effective marketing campaign aimed at the clients you most want. If someone outside that market shows up in your pipeline, by all means  do business with them. But focus your outgoing efforts on filling the pipeline with those clients you are most interested in getting.

It's important to base your target market description on demographics or industry classifications rather than the presumed need of a client for your service. A contract trainer specializing in conflict resolution skills, for example, would find little value in defining her target market as "organizations that experience conflict." This could be anyone.

"Organizations in need of conflict resolution training" won't do the job as a definition either. Could you look them up in a directory? Would a referral partner know who would be a good lead for you? Could you figure out where these people would go to network? No. You can't do any of these things with a need-based definition.

But if the trainer defined her market as "human resources development or training managers in midsize to large companies located in the Boston area," now she can find them, and so can her referral partners.

If your target market is organizations, here are some ways you could define them:

*Classification* (e.g., retailer, manufacturer, government agency)

*Industry* (e.g., health care, high tech, travel)

*Size* (by number of employees or annual revenue)

*Geographical location*

*Special characteristics* (e.g., well established, rapidly growing, family friendly)

*Decision makers* (by department, division, or position title)

And here are some ways to define individuals as prospective clients:

*Age*

*Gender*

*Family status* (e.g., married, children, aging parents)

*Occupation* (e.g., student, manager or executive, self-employed professional)

*Income* (by individual or household)

*Education* (e.g., high school, college, postgraduate)

*Geographical location*

*Interests and hobbies* (e.g., sports enthusiast, active investor, entertains often)

A final word of advice: you are better off defining two or three different target markets than one generic target intended to include them all. A financial planner seeking high-income individuals, for example, might choose "executives, established professionals, and successful entrepreneurs" as targeted groups. A definition like this is more helpful in locating prospects than saying "income over $100K."

## 10-Second Introduction

Your 10-second introduction is what you say when you shake someone's hand, call someone on the phone, or stand up in front of a group. It describes what you do and who you do it for in a clear and memorable way. One effective format is the *benefits-oriented introduction*, where you state the key benefit of your service before giving your occupation or job title. Here are some examples, beginning with one I often use:

> "My name is C. J. Hayden. I teach business owners and salespeople to make more money with less effort. I'm a business coach. The name of my company is Wings."

> "I'm Susan Schwartz, and I help real people get dressed. My business is U: A Personal Design Service, and I'm a personal style consultant."

> "My name is Barbara McDonald, and I'll help your business get noticed. I'm a graphic designer. My company is Native Design."

The advantage of this format is that it positions you in the mind of the listeners before they have a chance to form their own opinions about what you do. If you introduce yourself as an attorney, for example, your listener may think you are a litigator, estate planner, or do criminal defense work, none of which helps you get clients if you do family law. An introduction that begins, "I work with people going through divorce to help them get what they're entitled to," is both specific and memorable.

Notice that all these introductions use plain language rather than industry jargon. Unless you know exactly who your listeners are and what vernacular they speak, use terms a 12-year-old would understand.

## Business Cards

The purpose of a business card is to facilitate communication, not to give a complete description of your services. Put just enough information on your card for people to remember what you do, but not so much that they have no reason to call you. If you turn your business card into a brochure, people won't call you to ask for one, nor will you have anything new to send them after you meet.

Include your name, company name if you have one, mailing address, phone, fax, e-mail address, and web site, if applicable. Don't clutter up your card with cell phone and pager numbers. You can put these numbers on your outgoing voice-mail message if they are essential.

If your company name makes it clear what you do, that's probably all you need. Otherwise, choose from *one* of the following ways to indicate your profession:

1. *Title or function* (e.g., event planner, business broker, change management consulting).

2. *Specialties*. List no more than three (e.g., employment law—employee relations—dispute resolution; errands—organizing—bookkeeping; psychotherapy—consultation—training).

3. *Tag line* (e.g., "Strategic research in values and attitudes," "Helping nonprofits thrive," "Alleviating the stress of the information age").

The more expensive your service is, the more expensive your card should look, and the more likely you will need the services of a professional graphic designer. Adding color, a logo, or your photograph, using embossing, or choosing high-quality paper are all ways of improving the look of your card. If you will be relying on mailed information to impress prospective clients, your card will need to match the design of your letterhead, brochure, or marketing kit.

When you are marketing more than one business, you need more than one business card. Even if you find yourself giving both cards to the same person, they will represent what you offer much more clearly than if you try to put everything on the same card.

## Direct Contact and Follow-Up

### Calling and Mailing

*Success Ingredients*

prospect list

lead sources

Sending mailings and placing calls are activities more typical of the following-up stage than when filling the pipeline. This makes sense when you think about the whole purpose of your pipeline-filling activities: to find people you can call or mail to, or to get people to call you. So if you are working on filling the pipeline, you may be out of people to call.

But there are two situations where you may wish to call and mail to help get your pipeline full: contacting new people to see if they might become prospects, and contacting people you already know to stimulate referrals. (You'll find information about both of these subjects in Chapter 8 also.)

Whenever you contact someone new, the best approach is to call before you mail, and call again after you mail. Even if you don't reach the person on the first call, you can find out more information from his voice mail or the receptionist, and leave a message to expect something in the mail. On your postmailing call, if you again don't reach him, you can mention your letter, and prompt him to read it if he hasn't yet.

The purpose of your calls is twofold: to find out if this lead is actually a good prospect for you and, if so, to try to make a presentation. Remember that a presentation is simply the time when you tell your prospects what you can do for them. It's not necessarily anything formal and may even happen on the phone.

To accomplish your objectives, you will need to ask questions, not just give information. When you reach your prospect on the phone, begin with your 10-second introduction; then move immediately into conversation by asking a question. "Do you have a moment to talk about how I can help your company get better results from its training programs?" is a sample opening.

Be ready with two or three questions that will tell you immediately whether the person you are speaking with has a need for your service. If the need is there, ask for a meeting on the spot, or if you normally present by phone, do it right then. Don't back away by offering to send literature first. You may never get your prospect live on the phone again. Only if he declines to meet with you or to take time for your phone presentation should you offer to send something. This is also a polite way to end the conversation if the answers to your qualifying questions indicate this is not a prospect for you.

The people you might be calling if you are trying to fill the pipeline are probably those you looked up on a *prospect list* you purchased or found in a directory, or obtained from a *lead source*, such as the media or a networking pal. (See "Finding Prospects" below for more information.) The best kind of mail to send people like this is a personal letter. "Personal" means addressed to them by name and mentioning some situation that you have reason to believe exists and that you can help with. You can enclose a brochure or fact sheet, but don't send a lot of material. Wait for the follow-up stage to send anything more. And absolutely do follow up.

When contacting people you already know in order to fill the pipeline, you are hoping to encourage referrals by reminding them who you are and what you do. Those you contact might be former clients, people you have presented to in the past who didn't buy, or networking contacts.

You might choose to get in touch with these people by phone, and place a "what's new?" call. With center-of-influence types or likely referral partners, you might wish to schedule coffee or lunch. An easy way to contact a larger number of people, though, is by mail. Again, personal mailings have more impact than mass mailings of postcards or newsletters. An article, cartoon, or event announcement with a simple "thought you would be interested" note is friendly and effective.

## Meeting People in Person

Getting out of your office to meet people in person can be a welcome break from calling and mailing. (There's lots more information about this under "Networking and Referral Building" below.) Keep in mind, though, that you don't have to go to an official networking event to meet people. You meet new people all the time—at the grocery store, corner café, or dentist's office. Do all these people know what you do for a living?

Get in the habit of carrying your business cards everywhere. Whenever you meet someone, use your 10-second introduction, offer a business card, and ask for the other person's. You may feel awkward about this at first, but if you keep it up, it will soon become natural. If your service is primarily marketed to individuals rather than organizations—wedding planning, chiropractic, or home repair, for example—this informal way of meeting new prospects can be very successful.

And don't rule out this tactic if you market to organizations. All organizations are run by human beings, after all. That guy on the jogging path may turn out to be Charles Schwab, and the woman ahead of you in the espresso line might be Jessica McClintock.

## Finding Prospects

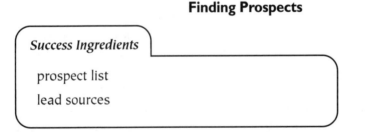

*Success Ingredients*

prospect list

lead sources

The best way to find prospects is by using the pipeline-filling strategies described later in this chapter. But locating prospective clients through research can be quite straightforward if you have done a good job defining your target market.

If you need a large number of prospects, you can purchase a targeted *prospect list* from a professional list broker (look in the Yellow Pages or search the Internet for "Mailing Lists"). For smaller numbers, particularly when marketing to businesses, it may be more affordable to create your own list from sources like those that follow, many of which you can purchase on disk or, for one-time or infrequent use, find in your local library.

> "There's a lot of information available for free," points out list broker Lisa Bowen, "but you have to consider the cost of using it too. Making photocopies at the library or sitting there punching names into your laptop gets old pretty quick. You can buy an already-compiled list for as little as $250. If you choose the one-year unlimited-use option, you can get a list already on disk and put it into your contact management system. This is absolutely worth it in terms of productivity. Instead of working on compiling the list, you can get on the phone.
>
> "It's easy to find a list of companies that fit your profile, but it's difficult with a compiled business list to get the names of all the marketing directors or all the human resources directors. You have to call up and ask, 'Who is the person responsible for...?' If you can't find a list that's exactly what you need, buy the closest match. It's much easier than compiling a list from scratch.
>
> "One of the best sources of information is professional associations. If they don't sell their list on disk, pay the membership fee, then turn over the membership directory to a data entry service. You can have the whole directory keyed in for as little as thirty cents a name.
>
> "Keep in mind the difference between prospects and suspects. *Prospects* are people you have talked to, so you and they both know they need your services. *Suspects* are people you think need you, but they don't know it yet. When you buy a list, you are getting suspects. To turn them into prospects, you have to make the calls.
>
> "The names on business lists turn over about 40 percent a year, so don't get more names than you can use in a calendar quarter. Frequently when you call someone, you find out they've moved on. But you do get a good list of companies. The ideal thing would be to get to the point where you already know all the companies in your area and you just update the names."
>
> Lisa Bowen, list broker, Prospects to Go,
> www.prospectstogo.com

*Sources for Prospect Lists*

- Yellow Pages and other general advertising directories
- Trade association directories (e.g., Chamber of Commerce, Better Business Bureau)
- Professional association membership directories
- Business and industry directories (e.g., Dun and Bradstreet)
- "Book of Lists" from your local *Business Times* or *Business Journal*

You can also develop your own ongoing *lead sources*, which might be professional or trade associations, educational institutions, print or broadcast media, on-line forums, or networking buddies. Associations and schools produce publications and events that will keep you in touch with what's happening in the industry they focus on. Print and broadcast media and on-line forums like bulletin boards, listserves, and chats can do the same. The more targeted the periodical, program, or forum is to the market that interests you, the better.

The people who are speaking at these events, writing expert articles, participating on-line, and being interviewed are all potential leads for you. Make note of any names or affiliations you see or hear from these sources. Finding out how to contact the person afterward is the easy part.

## A Word About Fear

It is completely normal to feel apprehensive about calling strangers on the phone. You have no idea how your call is going to be received, and if the person on the other end refuses to speak with you or isn't interested, it's hard not to take it personally. You may not even realize that you are afraid of making cold calls, but somehow, mysteriously, a hot lead will sit on your desk day after day and you just won't get around to picking up the phone.

Try asking yourself, "What is the worst thing that could possibly happen if I made that call?" Would it be hearing, "Don't bother me," or "Not interested"? Or would it be worse if the person you called was interested and you got tongue-tied and lost the sale? You know, though, that if you don't place the call, you've lost the sale anyway. So how bad could making the call really be?

The fact is that most people are polite in their refusals. They say, "No, thank you," and hang up. And when someone is interested in what you have to offer, the conversation gets easy pretty quickly; your prospect may actually help you along.

So what do you think: Can you pick up the phone? You'll never know what you are missing out on unless you make the call.

"One trick I teach to my clients who need to market themselves by phone is to change their physical posture. By habit, most of us do our business telephoning while sitting at our desks. But if you choose a different location or position, it can better support you in making challenging calls.

"If feeling more assertive or confident is what you need, make those calls standing up or walking around. If you find yourself sounding too pushy or talking too fast, try relaxing your body more; lean back in your chair, and cross your legs. If you're afraid of not having the right answers, be prepared with responses to predictable objections and questions, and assume a posture of alertness and focus by sitting up straight and keeping your head high.

"Clear your desk of distracting files and papers, and let your chair support your whole body. Some people need to clutch the phone as a prop, and others find freedom and flexibility using a headset or long cord. Experiment until you find what works best. You really can overcome your fears about marketing by phone by manipulating your environment, equipment, and your body."

Breeze Carlile, Certified Professional and Personal Coach,
WindDance Professional Coaching,
www.winddancecoaching.com

## Networking and Referral Building

### Attending Events

> *Success Ingredients*
>
> networking venues
> networking skills

Meeting people at organized events is one of the easiest and most effective ways to fill your marketing pipeline—easy, that is, if you're not afraid of talking to strangers. All you have to do is match your target market definition with the member profile of an existing association, organization, or institution, get on their mailing list, and go shake hands.

The places where you go to meet people are your *networking venues*.

### Popular Choices for Networking Venues

- Chamber of Commerce mixers, workshops, and award ceremonies
- Service clubs such as Rotary and Kiwanis
- Trade and professional association meetings where your clients are likely to gather
- Trade and professional association meetings where your referral partners are likely to gather
- Lectures, workshops, conferences, and fund raisers hosted by educational institutions, community organizations, and affinity groups
- Social, cultural, and sporting events that include receptions or other mix-and-mingle time
- Private gatherings organized for the purpose of meeting new people and schmoozing
- Lead exchange groups, where people in noncompetitive businesses gather weekly or monthly to swap leads and referrals

The best venues for networking are those intended to be a place for people to meet. If you attend a function like this, you can be assured that saying hello to someone you don't know will be accepted and welcome. Just walk up to anyone who looks interesting, stick out your hand, and say, "Hi, I haven't met you yet." Give the person your 10-second introduction and ask what he or she does.

If you are naturally shy, you may find that groups with a more structured format work better for you than informal mixers and receptions. Many networking events offer "introductions," which means that all members get a chance to stand up and tell the whole group what they do. Attendees may also be able to display or distribute flyers about their business. Even more structured than this is a lead exchange group.

Where do you find groups and events like this? Start by asking around. Anyone who is a likely referral partner for you can probably suggest some. Here are some other places you can look:

- Yellow Pages. Look under "Associations" or "Professional Organizations."
- Regional and local newspapers. Look for a "Business Calendar" or "Community Calendar" section.
- Chamber of Commerce. Ask for a list of local business and community organizations.

- *Business Times* or *Business Journal* for your metropolitan area.
- Specialized publications aimed at your target market's profession or area of special interest.
- Web sites that list events. Do a keyword search for your city (e.g., "Boston events").

In looking for events to attend, keep in mind that the way to get the most value from a group is to be a member of it. You will have more success in your networking if you go back to the same groups over and over than if you keep going to new groups all the time. Find two or three that seem to have the right mix of people, and keep going back.

So what if you are uncomfortable talking to strangers? Acquiring good *networking skills* will benefit you in all areas of your marketing. It's important to learn to introduce yourself smoothly, start a conversation with someone you don't know, and be comfortable in talking about your business in social settings. You might try practicing with friends, look for a workshop you could take, or read one of the many books on networking or mingling.

## Following Up With Contacts

If you don't follow up with the people you meet, you are wasting your time in meeting them. It is simply untrue that someone will call when they have a need for you. The truth is that if they have met you only once, they probably don't even remember you, and it's even less likely that they will remember where they put your card.

In this key area, marketing truly is telling people what you do, over and over. There is much more about follow-up in the next chapter, but the focus here is on how to follow up immediately with the people you meet at an event.

Take all those business cards out of your pocket and sort them into three piles: prospective clients, useful networking contacts, and other. Now sort the client pile into hot, warm, and cold leads. Stop right there and follow up with all the hot and warm leads. Call each one on the phone, reintroduce yourself, and try to make a presentation or get an appointment for one. If directly soliciting business is inappropriate in your profession (psychotherapy, for example), you can still make contact, perhaps with a "nice-to-meet-you" note. When you get voice mail or if someone requests more information, send a letter with a fact sheet or brochure. Put the person on your calendar for the next follow-up.

Next, go to the networking contacts and sort them into two piles: people who can lead you directly to prospective clients and people who can lead you to other marketing opportunities, such as a new networking group or a speaking engagement. Stop and follow up with the people who might have leads for you. Call them to suggest coffee or lunch, or offer to stop by the office.

You should now have three stacks of cards left: cold client leads, people who can lead you to marketing opportunities, and other. If you are short on time or have other hot leads in the pipeline, send those cold leads a nice-to-meet-you note, and tuck them away in your contact management system in case you need them later. If the new marketing opportunities fit into your current plans, go ahead and call those people. Otherwise treat them just like the cold leads.

And those "other" cards? Throw them away. If they aren't worth following up with, they don't belong in your contact management system.

---

Success coach Caterina Rando says she built her business largely through networking. Here are her suggestions for getting the most from attending events:

1. *Arrive early and stay late.* Better yet, volunteer to help for a portion of the event, but only a portion.

2. *Introduce yourself to as many people as possible.* Have a strong handshake, and make eye contact. Wear your name tag on the right-hand side, so people see it when you are shaking hands. Deliver your benefits-oriented introduction. Make sure they understand what you do.

3. *Engage in conversation with each person you meet.* Remember you are creating a relationship. Ask questions about them and their business; find out what their needs are. Communicate your wants and needs; give examples of who would be a good customer for you.

4. *Exchange business cards.* Offer yours, and ask for theirs. It's more important to get theirs than to give them yours. If they don't have a card, ask them to write down their name and phone number on one of yours. Put your business cards in one pocket and the ones you collect in another. You don't want to hand out someone else's card instead of your own.

5. *End the conversation with a commitment.* Before you move on, communicate an action you will take: "I'll send you that information," "I'll call you with so-and-so's number," or "I'll see you here next time." Don't let any one conversation go on too long.

6. *Write down what you said you would do.* As soon as you walk away, note any promise you made on the back of the person's card. Also note anything you want to remember about the conversation. Later you won't be able to recall what was said.
   Caterina Rando, Certified Professional and
   Personal Coach and speaker, www.CaterinaR.com

## Networking With Referral Partners

> *Success Ingredient*
>
> referral partners

A *referral partner* is a person, group, or institution willing to refer potential clients to you. Building relationships with referral partners can be a powerful way to fill your marketing pipeline. If enough people begin referring business to you, you will eventually achieve the enviable position of being able to respond to client inquiries instead of having to initiate contact yourself.

A prospective client who is referred to you is much more likely to buy what you have to sell than someone who hasn't been referred. The endorsement of the person making the referral carries a lot of weight, increasing the know-like-and-trust factor immediately. Referred prospects are less likely to shop for the lowest price, ask fewer questions about your background and expertise, and typically come to a decision much more quickly. If soliciting business is inappropriate in your profession, referrals may be your primary source of clients.

For all these reasons, concentrating some effort on building referrals can be a very worthwhile use of your time. While some of the best referrals come from past clients, there are many other possible referral partners for any business.

### Possible Referral Partners

• *Other prospects.* People you have spoken to or met with but aren't ready to buy from you now will still refer you to others, if you remember to keep in touch with them.

• *Colleagues.* Others in your field can be excellent referral sources. If you offer noncompetitive services, you may even approach prospective clients together.

• *Competitors.* Don't rule out your competitors as referral partners. You may have an area of specialty that they don't. They may also have times when they can't handle all the business that comes to them or can't take on a particular client because of a conflict of interest.

• *Others who serve your market.* Anyone who is in regular contact with your target market is a potential referral partner, regardless of the field. A computer network installer might easily collect referrals from the owner of a moving company, a commercial property manager, or a security systems salesperson—all people who might know about an upcoming office relocation.

• *Salespeople*. Regardless of what they sell, salespeople are used to the process of giving and receiving referrals. If you make friends with someone who sells for a living, he or she will naturally be on the lookout for possible leads for you. Start with the salespeople who sell to you.

• *Centers of influence*. These are the people everyone seems to know. You see them at networking events, read their names in the trade press, and hear their names mentioned everywhere. People like this get asked for referrals all the time, so you want your name to be in their contact management system.

• *Organizations*. When a prestigious nonprofit or educational institution refers you, it is an implied endorsement and makes you very attractive to prospective customers. Building relationships with organizations like this typically requires volunteering your professional services or teaching for them.

To begin identifying potential referral partners, develop a list of categories that represents the type of people or groups you think would be good candidates. For example, if you were an executive recruiter specializing in start-ups and rapidly growing small companies, your referral partner categories might be:

- Accountants who serve this market
- Attorneys specializing in stock offerings, contracts, patents, trademarks, and other relevant areas
- Business development consultants
- Business and investment bankers
- Entrepreneurship centers
- Human resources management consultants
- Marketing consultants
- Venture capitalists

When you have identified some promising categories, look through your existing contacts to see who fits. Call those people up, and say, "You know, I think we may be able to help each other get more clients. Can we get together and talk about it?" After you have contacted the people you already know, you can add to your circle of referral partners by employing the same strategies you are using to discover and attract clients.

The best referral partnerships are reciprocal. If the two of you are operating in the same target market, the possibility of referrals' flowing both ways is quite high. But even if you can't imagine how you would be able to refer business to the person you are contacting, don't let that stop you. Savvy businesspeople are always looking for qualified professionals to add to their referral bank, because it helps them take good care of their own clients.

When you meet with a potential referral partner, find out as much about the partner's business as you tell her about yours. Exchange marketing litera-ture and several business cards. Ask who would be a good referral for your partner, and explain what type of client you are looking for. End your conver-sation by asking, "Is there anything else you need to feel confident in referring prospective clients to me?"

Be sure to thank your partners for each and every referral, whether it turns into business for you or not. Prompt thank-yous will generate more referrals. Keep in touch with your partners over time, just as you do with prospective and former clients. And remember to be on the lookout for referrals you can give to your partners. That's the best way possible to stay in touch with them.

## Networking on the Web

The skyrocketing use of the Internet has created a number of new ways to net-work without leaving your office. If you subscribe to one of the major on-line services, there may be an entire area dedicated to your profession or target market. Making a keyword search of the World Wide Web for sites related to your profession, market, or area of expertise will point you to many more pos-sibilities. Here are some of the ways you can use the Web to network:

• *Bulletin boards.* Most sites and areas contain one or more bulletin boards where you can post questions and comments on a specific subject. Answering a posted question is an excellent way to demon-strate your expertise. Don't be overly self-promotional. Just include a brief identifier in your signature line, such as "Margo Komenar, author of *Electronic Marketing.*"

• *Live chats.* Interactive discussion groups exist for almost any topic you can imagine. Participating in these chats is an excellent way to meet people interested in the subject being discussed.

• *Listserves.* These contain postings, questions, and comments on a specific subject or of interest to a particular group, and are e-mailed to all the group members daily, weekly, or whenever a new posting arrives. Discussion threads on a hot topic are common on these lists. You can quickly start your own thread by e-mailing a provocative question to a group of interested people, and instructing them to choose Reply to All when they respond.

Before participating in any of these forums, spend some time observing how the existing members tend to communicate. When you have a good sense of the accepted protocol, start making your own contributions.

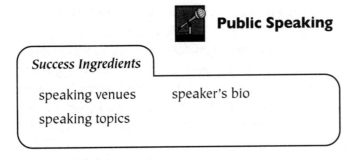

**Public Speaking**

*Success Ingredients*

speaking venues     speaker's bio

speaking topics

Speaking in public creates positive visibility, boosts your credibility, and establishes you as an expert in your field. It puts you in direct contact with potential clients in such a powerful way that you may find yourself closing a sale before leaving the room. With all the benefits public speaking offers, it's unfortunate that surveys show most people are more afraid of speaking in public than of dying.

If this is true for you, don't include public speaking on your list of strategies just yet. You want to make a good impression on your prospective clients, and you're not going to do it if you're quaking in your boots. Work on getting some practice first. The fact is that the only way to reduce the fear of public speaking is to get experience speaking in public.

Try taking a class at your local community college, or from a private training organization such as Dale Carnegie. Join a local Toastmasters group, where people meet regularly to practice their speaking and get feedback on their delivery. Or look for a Speaking Circle in your area. These are groups led by trained facilitators that assist you in developing a natural and authentic speaking style.

You can work more gradually on becoming a public speaker by participating in a networking or lead exchange group that requires all members to introduce themselves at every meeting. Your next step might be volunteering to host part of a program or make announcements for a networking group you are part of. After that, you might be ready to serve on a panel, where it is common to speak while staying seated and referring to notes.

Over time, you will get more comfortable at being in front of a group and be able to carry off a 20-minute talk without experiencing panic. You may even grow to like public speaking, and graduate to conducting a 90-minute breakout session at a conference or even a three-hour workshop. The more value someone receives from your presentation, the more likely that person is to become a client.

When you are ready to get started with speaking to promote your business, you will first need to locate some *speaking venues*. These are the places, groups, or events where you can give free presentations to prospective clients or referral partners. "Free" doesn't mean there is no admission charge. It means that you, the speaker, are not being paid, although in some cases you may receive an honorarium.

**Possible Speaking Venues**

- Chamber of Commerce networking events and workshops
- Service clubs such as Rotary and Kiwanis
- Trade and professional association meetings and conferences
- Lectures, workshops, and conferences hosted by educational institutions, community organizations, and affinity groups
- Classes offered by community colleges, resource centers, and private learning centers such as the Learning Annex
- Live chats hosted by on-line services and web sites

If some of the entries on this list look suspiciously like those on the list of suggested places to network, you have noticed something very important! Public speaking is superpowered networking. You can speak to the same groups you might otherwise just visit, and you can find them using some of the same resources mentioned in the section on networking and referral building. But as the speaker, you will be standing in front of the room instead of sitting in the audience.

To approach a group about being a speaker, you will need to develop one to three *speaking topics* you would like to present. Your topics should be interesting and distinctive, and show off your specialized expertise. They should also allow you to tell stories about your work and include examples of what you have done for clients. In this way, you can deliver value to your audience and promote yourself effectively at the same time.

Most networking groups, service clubs, and professional organizations give their guest speakers between 20 and 60 minutes for their talk. Breakout sessions, workshops, and classes can run from 90 minutes to three hours, or even a full day. You may wish to choose topics that can be expanded if you find an opportunity for a longer program, or just stick to topics suitable for a short talk. Be sure to give your topics enticing titles that will attract plenty of prospects when printed in a group's newsletter or program flyer.

Write brief descriptions of each topic that will give group organizers enough information to decide if they like it, and can also be used to promote your talk once it is scheduled. Here's a sample topic description for one of my own popular talks:

### *Overcoming the Fear of Self-Promotion*

What is it that makes you hesitate to broadcast your accomplishments and capabilities? Is it merely that you were taught bragging is impolite, or is there something else going on? Reluctance to promote yourself holds you back from achieving personal fulfillment and financial success. You can vanquish this fear and learn to promote yourself effectively! Available as a short talk, half-day, or full-day seminar.

Being the guest speaker for an on-line chat works a bit differently. Rather than delivering a presentation, you serve as an expert resource for the people participating. You typically begin the chat with a few prepared remarks, and then take questions from the participants, one at a time. To get booked for a chat, it's more important to impress the producer with your expertise than to have a well-developed topic. Be sure to attend a few chats before you speak for one, and brush up on your typing skills.

The final essential tool for getting yourself booked as a speaker is a *speaker's bio* to accompany your topic descriptions. This can be the same professional biography you might print on a brochure or include in a marketing kit (see Chapter 8), with one important addition: include any prior speaking experience you have.

If you have only given one or two presentations, you might just add a line to your bio like, "Carlos Maldonado's presentations have been well received by organizations such as the Miami Independent Computer Consultants Association and the South Florida Technology Consortium." If your speaking experience is more extensive, consider listing the places you have spoken at the bottom of your bio page or even on a separate sheet.

If you have never spoken in public and have no credits to list on your bio, don't let that stop you. If you believe you can do a good job, go for it. You have to give your first talk sometime.

With your topic descriptions and bio prepared, you are ready to start approaching your chosen venues. For networking groups, service clubs, and association meetings, typically you will need to contact the program chair, who is often a volunteer working out of his or her own home or office. It's a good idea to find out something about the group before you place that call. You want to make sure the audience is right for you and be able to tell the chairperson why your topic would be of interest.

Call the group's main number or membership chair, and ask for information about the group and its upcoming events. Most groups will mail you an information packet or newsletter. This will tell you more about the group and probably also give you the program chair's name. If you still think this group is

"The most common response I hear when a successful businessperson is asked to speak is, 'What would I talk about?'" reports Roseann Sullivan. The principal of a promotional communications training and consulting firm, Roseann helps her clients "become someone everyone knows."

Roseann suggests, "Talk about the things people ask you about at parties. What aspect of your work do you find yourself spending hours of your free time discussing? What information do you have that can solve people's problems? A tax attorney could talk about winning an audit and a publicist about getting free publicity.

"Don't talk about anything that bores you. A topic you are interested in is going to be much easier for you to write and deliver. Motivational speaker Napoleon Hill said, 'Enthusiasm is the radio wave by which you transmit your personality to others.' If you want them to like you, you have to be enthusiastic about your subject.

"Think beyond the predictable. Too many unknowing professionals waste time and money developing overdone presentations. For example, if you are a realtor, avoid the temptation to give a predictable presentation on buying your first home. Do something different, like 'how to escape the big city.' Unconventional topics will draw crowds of prospects to your program.

"When deciding on your topic and approach, focus on giving valuable information and exceeding the expectations of your audience. Impart some wisdom to them, so that even if they don't become your clients, your presentation makes an impact. Create goodwill by always giving 110 percent. You already know the importance of word-of-mouth marketing, so make sure there are lots of good words floating around about you."

Roseann Sullivan, promotional communications
consultant and speaker, Speaking for
Your Success, www.speak2u.com

an appropriate venue for you, get the program chair's number and make your pitch by phone. Don't waste your time sending information to the group's main mailing address; it will probably be discarded.

If the program chairperson expresses interest, find out how far ahead the group is scheduling speakers, and send the chairperson your topics and bio. Then follow up after an appropriate interval to see if you are able to get yourself on the program.

With educational institutions, resource centers, and private learning centers, study the catalog before you call. If they already have a class on your topic, see if you can find a new and different angle that hasn't yet been covered. When you're sure you have something fresh to propose, call the department chair or program director to see if the organization is interested. You will probably be asked to submit a proposal, for which the group may or may not have written guidelines. If no guidelines are available, send a description of your proposed topic and speaker's bio, with a cover letter explaining why you think this topic will be popular with the audience. And don't forget to follow up.

 **Writing and Publicity**

## Writing Articles About Your Specialty

*Success Ingredients*

writing venues

writing query

Just like public speaking, writing expert articles can help you become more credible as well as more visible. A well-written article on a subject of interest to your target market will get their attention, demonstrate your expertise, and increase your name recognition. Once your article is published, you can also use it as a marketing tool in a wide variety of ways.

### Getting Mileage From Articles You've Written

- Include copies of the article in your marketing kit or press kit.
- Send copies to people on your follow-up list with a "thought-you-would-be-interested" note attached.
- Send copies to your clients with your next invoice.
- Use it as a handout when you speak to a group, or offer to send it to anyone who gives you his or her business card.
- Leave it behind with prospects when you make a presentation.
- Frame the original, and hang it on your office wall.

The first step in getting an expert article published is to identify appropriate *writing venues*. What do the people in your target market read? Consider newsletters (print or e-mail), magazines, trade journals, and newspapers. Ask your clients and prospects what publications they subscribe to or regularly buy. Notice which periodicals are lying on their desks and poking out of their briefcases. You can also look up possible venues in directories of writing markets, such as those published by Writer's Digest Books.

If you are new to getting your writing published, start with small publications that don't require writing experience. Association newsletters are an excellent first target. Other possibilities are employee newsletters for companies you would like as clients, promotional newsletters or web sites produced by your referral partners, community newspapers, or advertising periodicals, like those that list homes for sale or job openings.

When you have a venue in mind, compose a *writing query*. Smaller publications can be queried by phone, but larger ones usually require a written query. If you're not sure, call the appropriate editor and ask. Most publications list the name and department of each editor in a box near the table of contents, inside the front cover, or for newspapers, in the editorial section.

If you contact the editor by phone, be prepared to pitch your article idea on the spot. Describe your proposed topic, explain why it is of interest to readers, and tell why you should be the one who writes it. If you're convincing enough, a small publication might give you the assignment right there. A larger one will probably ask you to send a query letter and include some clips of your writing.

Don't try to skip the query step by sending a completed article in the hope that the publication will print it. Most editors won't even look at it, and you will have wasted a great deal of time. There are some exceptions to this rule— guest editorials are one example—but in these cases, the publication will have clearly stated guidelines about the length and format of articles it will accept.

A query letter should begin with a strong lead paragraph, written just as if it were the opening paragraph of the actual article. You want it to capture the editor's interest, introduce your topic, and show that you can write. Continue the letter by describing two or three key points you intend to have your article make. Then propose the article itself: "I would like to write a 1,500-word article on the benefits to employers of integrated disability management programs. I plan to interview three employers who have experienced significant cost reductions..."

Conclude the letter with a brief description of your background that indicates why you are qualified to write the article. If you have previously been published, send along two sample articles with your letter. Be sure to send a self-addressed stamped envelope if you are querying by mail. E-mail submissions are becoming more common, but don't use this method unless you know it is acceptable.

The elapsed time it takes editors to respond to a query varies widely. Unless you have been told otherwise, follow up after 30 days if you haven't heard anything. This is particularly important because you shouldn't send the same query to another editor until you are sure the first one doesn't want your article.

Once you successfully place a number of articles, you might consider finding a venue for an ongoing column. Landing a regular column in a publication respected by your target market is a major milestone in establishing your expertise, and can significantly boost your name recognition.

## Getting Media Publicity

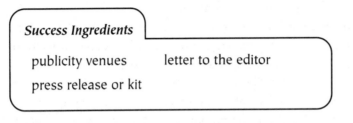

*Success Ingredients*

publicity venues        letter to the editor

press release or kit

Attracting the attention of the print and broadcast media can get you quoted, interviewed, or profiled. When prospective clients see you featured in the news, your credibility and name recognition may greatly increase. The more visible you are in your profession, the more likely it is that the media will contact you, but don't just sit back and wait. Generating publicity can be relatively easy, particularly if you start with smaller outlets.

Begin by identifying the best *publicity venues*—places your target market or referral partners will be likely to notice an article or interview about you. Here are some suggestions, beginning with some of the easier targets for your first publicity attempt:

*Potential Publicity Venues*

- Newsletter of a professional association or networking group of which you are a member

- Alumni newsletter for your school or college

- Newsletter of an organization you volunteer for

- Local newspaper for your neighborhood or town

- Local trade journal for your profession

- Local radio or cable television show that focuses on a topic in your area of expertise

- Local or regional magazine that covers topics you can speak to

- Daily newspaper for your metropolitan area

- Local television news, magazine, or talk show

- National trade journal for your profession

- National magazine that covers topics you can speak to

- Nationally syndicated radio show

- National wire service (e.g., Associated Press, Knight-Ridder)

- National print news media (e.g., *Newsweek, Wall Street Journal*)

- National television news, magazine, or talk show

For newsletters, magazines, and newspapers, you will need the name of the appropriate editor. For radio and television, you will need the appropriate producer's name. For news media, you can also approach reporters who cover the topic you are seeking publicity about. You can usually get these names by reading, watching, or listening to the publication or program you plan to approach (which is a good idea anyway). You can also look them up in directories like *Bacon's Publicity Checker.*

An essential tool for approaching the media is a well-written *press release,* which may be one component of a complete *press kit.* A press release is a one- or two-page bulletin that you send to the media to pitch your story. Successful releases issued by small business owners and professionals generally fall into one of three categories:

1. *News.* You are announcing something that the venues you are approaching will consider newsworthy. For an association newsletter or neighborhood newspaper, this might be the opening of your business or landing a new client. For larger media, you need bigger news, such as publication of a book or survey, an invention or discovery, or winning an award. If you don't have a major event like this to announce, don't despair. Consider what kind of problems your clients are experiencing that you can solve. Is there a potential news story in these problems?

2. *Commentary.* This type of release is positioning you as an expert who would be great to interview on a currently hot topic. "Sandwich Generation Feeling the Squeeze" could be the headline for a geriatric care consultant's release. Begin with a pithy quote (your own!) on the chosen subject, describe the situation that makes your comments topical, and give a brief summary of your expertise.

3. *Miniarticle.* Many publications will print your press release verbatim if it is written in the form of a brief article of high interest to their readers. Articles with a seasonal angle can be very successful. A per-

sonal shopper might write 300 words on "Buying Lingerie for Your Valentine," with herself as the expert quoted in the article.

Figure 7-1 shows a sample press release of the news variety to show you the format and style the media expects.

When you are angling for a feature article or live interview, you may want to supplement your press release with other material, turning it into a complete press kit. This should be sent to media contacts only after they have expressed some interest. You might include a one-page biography of yourself or profile of your company, a photograph (action photos are best), clips of other press you have received, an article you had published, or a list of sample questions and answers for an interview. An audiotape or videotape of a previous interview can also help impress producers.

**Figure 7-1. Sample press release.**

---

For Release: March 20, 1999 Contact: Barbara McDonald
Phone: 510/658-7618

SELF-TAUGHT DESIGNER WINS BAY AREA LOGO DESIGN CONTEST

A logo created by Oakland-based graphic designer Barbara McDonald was chosen over more than 250 entries received in a design contest sponsored by the San Francisco Foundation. The contest, open to Bay Area artists of all types, challenged entrants to design a new logo for The San Francisco Foundation, an organization beginning its fiftieth year of service to Bay Area communities.

The San Francisco Foundation, which awards grants to nonprofit organizations in economic development, education, environment, culture, immigration, and youth, awarded McDonald $6,000 for her winning entry and will use it on all of its printed materials, signage, and web site. "I was thrilled to have just made it to the finals of the contest," said McDonald, "but then to have my logo chosen by a prestigious organization like the San Francisco Foundation was quite an honor for me."

A self-taught artist, McDonald started her career painting sets and props for the Disney Design Center, then moved into graphic design while working for a large sign company in Los Angeles. Her business, Native Design, was founded in 1994, and her clients range from small business owners like herself to local restaurants like Picante and Jupiter, and medium-sized companies like the California Academy of Family Physicians.

"It has always been important for me to work with people and organizations who make a positive contribution to the community, and the San Francisco Foundation is the epitome of that type of client," stated McDonald.

---

As you should always do when approaching prospective clients, call your media contacts before sending them a release. Pitch your story on the spot, and try to interest them. If they do want your release, ask how they would like to receive it. If it seems appropriate, send your whole press kit.

If you want to blanket the media with your story and can't afford the time and money to make all those phone calls, be sure to send your release by mail rather than fax. Unsolicited faxes are rarely read. The blanket approach can work well for releases in the miniarticle style, but for news or commentary releases, your story must be extremely compelling to get the media's attention.

One final way to get visibility in the media is to write a *letter to the editor*. Commenting on a published piece or broadcast story can get your letter printed or read on the air. It can also get you into the editor's or producer's contact database. Conclude your letter with a paragraph like this: "The next time you cover a story on home offices or telecommuting, please feel free to contact me for background information. I am a professional organizer who specializes in helping home-based workers run their offices efficiently." Enclose your business card or, better yet, a card for their rotary file with a tab saying "Home Office/Telecommuting."

 **Promotional Events**

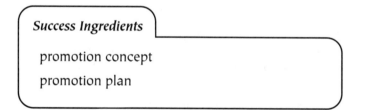

*Success Ingredients*

promotion concept

promotion plan

Organizing or participating in a promotional event can consume a significant amount of time and money. Before making a commitment to put on a show, check your budget. Add up all the costs of producing the event, promoting it, and making a good showing at it. Divide the total by the number of clients you can honestly expect to get as a result of the event, to see how much each client is going to cost you. Do you still think it's worth it? Can you think of an easier or cheaper way to get the same number of clients?

Only if your event passes this test should you go ahead with it. Many service business owners have found exhibit booths at trade shows to be an expensive mistake. On the other hand, free demonstrations or low-cost workshops have been a solid source of clients for many consultants and professionals. Ask your colleagues what has worked, and not worked, for them.

"In public relations, your job is to define your expertise to the media," advises public relations and marketing consultant Jill Lublin. "One of my clients is an industrial designer for corporations—interesting but not exciting. It turns out he runs his successful company as a 'virtual corporation,' so he became an expert on that topic. That caught the media's attention, and he has been featured nationally in newspapers, radio, and television.

"Here are some key points to remember in using public relations:

"1. Be ready to define your business concisely. Prepare a 30-second introduction that includes your business, your name, and a benefit of doing business with you.

"2. Know who your public is, and target your audience. Yes, the universe can be your audience, but it's very expensive to market to. Define your audience with demographics.

"3. Tell your story. Why would someone want to do business with you? Find out what makes you the most interesting and relates to the largest amount of people.

"4. Write a press release that answers the who, what, where, when, and why of your story. A well-written, concise release with an exciting lead paragraph will increase your chances.

"5. Send your release to a researched media list. Have as many names as possible that are relevant to your topic, including business editors, features editors, columnists, and producers.

"6. Follow up your release with phone calls. Have alternative pitches ready in case your media contact doesn't like the first one. Be precise and to the point when leaving a message.

"The media are accessible. We, the public, create stories. What you see in the news is about people like you and me. Read the paper you will be talking to, watch the television show, or listen to the radio program to see where you can fit in to make some news of your own."

Jill Lublin, public relations and marketing
consultant, Promising Promotion,
www.PromisingPromotion.com

To create or be part of a promotional event, a *promotion concept* is the starting place.

### *Ideas for Promotional Events*

- A display table at your networking group's business fair or expo
- An exhibit booth at a trade show or community event attended by your target market
- Hosting a networking event or open house at your place of business
- Being a sponsor for a fund-raising event or award ceremony
- Demonstrating or exhibiting your work in your office or studio or at an outside event
- Offering a free or low-cost workshop to your target audience

When you have come up with a concept that you like and tested its financial viability, you're ready to make a *promotion plan*. The more elaborate your event is, the more extensive your planning needs. Here are some elements your plan might include:

• *Advance publicity*. Even if the event is sponsored by someone else, you will get more mileage from it if you invite prospects to attend. Many trade shows and fund raisers provide postcards or flyers for this purpose. If you are the sponsor, evaluate all the marketing techniques at your disposal to determine what combination might work the best. You may want to mail invitations, post flyers, issue press releases, or purchase ad space.

• *Exhibit booth*. Your booth or display table should reflect your level of professionalism and visually display your expertise. Use photographs, testimonial letters, sample reports, press clippings, and so forth to make what you do as tangible as possible. Try to find out what sort of displays any other exhibitors will have. You don't want to look cheap or unprepared by comparison.

• *Marketing literature*. If you exhibit at a large event, be prepared to give away many copies of your literature. Some attendees make a habit of taking something from each booth, regardless of whether they are actually interested. It's a good idea to have a relatively inexpensive piece available for the taking, and keep your more costly brochure or marketing kit behind the table to give to serious prospects.

• *Script or outline*. Prepare in advance what you will say to people who come by your booth. Think of one good qualifying question you can ask at the outset of a conversation to see if the person you are speaking with is a prospect. Write out a script for any helpers you plan to have so they can answer predictable questions. If you will be conducting a demonstration or workshop, script or outline it, and be sure to rehearse. You will be the star of this show, and you don't want to flop.

• *Capturing leads*. The traditional way to capture the contact information of people who attend an event is to collect their business cards for a drawing. This can result in a large number of cards, though, with no way of knowing who is a legitimate prospect. Insert a qualifier into your drawing: Ask people to answer a qualifying question on the back of their card before dropping it in. To save time at an exhibit booth, use two stickers of different colors to indicate yes or no.

• *Logistical details*. Plan ahead for all the small things that can make your event more successful—for example, extra helpers, refreshments, giveaways, pens and paper, small bills to make change, and name tags. If all the details are handled, you can concentrate on making a good impression.

 **Advertising**

There are a number of reasons that advertising is last on the list of marketing strategies for the service business. First, there's the know-like-and-trust factor. Advertising is not an effective way to get a prospective client's trust. Second, advertising generates leads, not sales. People calling you from an ad will take much more convincing than prospects who are referred to you. They will be more likely to bargain for a lower price, ask for references, or require a written proposal than will the people who already know you.

Third, like any other marketing strategy, advertising must be done repeatedly to have an effect. Ongoing advertising can be very expensive. H & R Block can afford to advertise their tax preparation services because they have an enormous staff in many locations waiting to serve customers. The cost of this advertising is reasonable when divided by that many people, all working to generate revenue. But a two-person accounting office can't generate enough revenue to pay for an extensive advertising campaign.

Finally, the other five strategies all work better than advertising for the vast majority of service businesses. Sure, advertising might work for you, but the idea is to get the best result with the least investment of time and money.

Advertising is an investment—a high-risk investment. In using it, you should follow the same steps as you would to invest in anything:

1. Analyze your options carefully.

2. Choose wisely.

3. Don't invest what you can't afford to lose.

Always look at the potential return on your investment:

- How many leads do you expect your ads to generate?

- What will each lead cost you?

- How many will become customers?

- What will be the dollar value of those closed sales?

- Is there a cheaper way you could generate the same amount of revenue?

- How much can you really afford to spend?

Keep in mind that all the advice in this book is about marketing services, not products. If you also have products for sale, you may find that advertising is not only helpful but necessary.

Once you have made the commitment to advertise, and know what you can afford to invest, here are some suggestions for getting the most from your advertising dollar:

- *Target the right audience.* The narrower your target, the better. Specialized publications are often cheaper than the ones with wide appeal. Targeting also permits you to tailor your ad for the people most likely to buy.

- *Place your ad where they "shop."* When is it most likely that a customer will realize she needs you? Where might she be looking when she is in the mood? If you owned a secretarial service targeting home business owners, you could advertise in your neighborhood newspaper and hope that the right people ran across your ad. But it's more likely that hot prospects would find you in the Yellow Pages.

- *Request an immediate response.* Institutional advertising is for the big guys. You really can't afford to advertise just for name recognition; you need a direct response. A computer consultant serving busy entrepreneurs might headline her ad: "How much time did you waste last month looking for missing paperwork? We can help. Call for our free guide to the almost-paperless office."

- *Repeat; don't scatter.* People often don't respond the first, second, or tenth time they see your ad, so give them more chances. When your budget is limited, buy repeat ads in the same publication, not one ad in several different ones. Make sure people see your ad often. For the

1. The first time a man looks at an advertisement, he does not see it.

2. The second time, he does not notice it.

3. The third time, he is conscious of its existence.

4. The fourth time, he faintly remembers having seen it before.

5. The fifth time, he reads it.

6. The sixth time, he turns up his nose at it.

7. The seventh time, he reads it through and says, "Oh brother!"

8. The eighth time, he says, "Here's that confounded thing again!"

9. The ninth time, he wonders if it amounts to anything.

10. The tenth time, he asks his neighbor if he has tried it.

11. The eleventh time, he wonders how the advertiser makes it pay.

12. The twelfth time, he thinks it must be a good thing.

13. The thirteenth time, he thinks perhaps it might be worth something.

14. The fourteenth time, he remembers wanting such a thing a long time.

15. The fifteenth time, he is tantalized because he cannot afford to buy it.

16. The sixteenth time, he thinks he will buy it some day.

17. The seventeenth time, he makes a memorandum to buy it.

18. The eighteenth time, he swears at his poverty.

19. The nineteenth time, he counts his money carefully.

20. The twentieth time he sees the ad, he buys what it is offering.

Written in 1885 by Thomas Smith, London, England

same money that a big display ad would cost once per quarter, you could probably run a classified once a week.

• *Track and adjust.* Keep track of the response to every ad—not just the volume of calls but the value of the sales they generate. To do this, you will need to keep accurate records of where every customer comes from and how much each spends with you. If an ad isn't bringing you paying customers after an extended run, dump it, even if you're getting plenty of inquiries. Revisit the points above, and see if you can come closer to your target, where they shop, and what will prompt a response. And if an ad is working for you, don't change it. You will get tired of your ads long before your customers do.

## Distributing Flyers

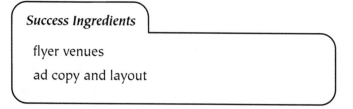

*Success Ingredients*

flyer venues

ad copy and layout

Flyers are one of the most inexpensive forms of advertising. If you are already doing a fair amount of networking and referral building, you may often find yourself in places where you can hand out, post, or display flyers to increase your visibility and generate new inquiries. Likely *flyer venues* include the following places:

• *Networking events.* You may be able to hand out flyers when you introduce yourself, leave them on a table for people to pick up, or place one on each chair. If you don't know what the group's rules are, be sure to ask first so you don't offend anyone.

• *Trade shows.* If you have a booth, your flyers will be there, of course. If you don't, you could ask a referral partner to display flyers for you. Most shows prohibit the distribution of flyers by nonexhibitors, but creative entrepreneurs have been known to hand out flyers outside the show.

• *Educational institutions, professional association headquarters, resource centers, and community gathering places.* Many have bulletin boards, resource binders, or literature racks where your flyers could be seen or picked up.

The *ad copy and layout* of your flyer will be important to its effectiveness. Special offers such as "mention this ad for a 15% discount" or "free consultation with this flyer" can encourage people to call. Flyers that advertise only one service at a time get more response than those that contain a laundry list of everything available.

The design and printing of your flyer should reflect your level of professionalism. If your flyer looks homemade, that's how people will view your service. Consider investing a few extra dollars in having your flyer professionally designed. For small quantities, good-quality photocopies will be more affordable than offset printing, but be sure the paper stock you use projects the image that you want.

## Direct Mail

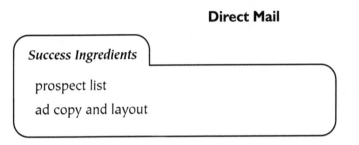

*Success Ingredients*

prospect list

ad copy and layout

The difference between direct mail and sending personal letters to prospective clients is the level of individual attention you give the prospect and the volume of marketing pieces you send. The difference in the impact these two tactics have can be significant. Think of yourself as an example. How much of the mail arriving at your door do you actually read? Do those marketing letters you get with your name inserted fool you into thinking the letter was written just for you?

Many people who receive a lot of mail routinely throw away envelopes from senders they don't recognize. If they do hang on to your mailing, it will probably be sitting at the bottom of a stack somewhere. This is why calling before you send a personal letter is so important. It may be the only way to save your letter from the circular file. And calling after you send it is the only way to know if it got read.

Sending a generic marketing piece to a large *prospect list* is better used as a follow-up technique than for filling the pipeline. (See the material about newsletters and postcards or mailers in Chapter 8.) If despite these warnings, you want to try using direct mail as your first approach to a cold list, consider working with a marketing communications specialist to design the *ad copy and layout* for your mailing. Getting professional help to compose your letter, design your mailer, or lay out your postcard can greatly increase its effectiveness.

Try offering a free gift, complimentary consultation, or other time-limited offer as an incentive for the recipient to call you. If you are sending a letter, paying someone to hand-address the envelopes is one way to increase the odds of the letter's being opened. Printing a teaser on the outside—"Look inside for your free gift"—is another. Just be sure whatever tricks you use to get your mailing piece noticed reflect the image you want to present.

## Directory Advertising

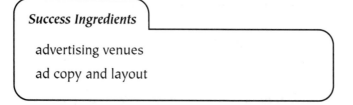

*Success Ingredients*

advertising venues

ad copy and layout

One of the most popular *advertising venues* for service businesses is the advertising directory. This category includes the Yellow Pages produced by your local phone company; similar directories produced by competing groups; membership directories and resource guides printed by associations, unions, and other trade groups; and affinity group directories, such as the Women's Yellow Pages.

There are really only two reasons to advertise in a particular directory:

1. You expect that potential customers will be looking for your service in that directory at the time they are ready to buy.

2. It is standard practice in your industry to be listed in that directory, so it would detract from your credibility if you weren't included.

When advertising solely for the second reason, there's no point in buying a big ad. Just pay for the basic listing. Don't worry about impressing potential buyers with the size of your ad. Even well-established companies often keep this type of ad quite small.

When you are advertising for reason 1, it's important that your *ad copy and layout* be designed to catch the eye of your best prospects. Study the existing ads in your category carefully. Make yours stand out by using unique graphics or an intriguing headline. If there are many large ads in your category already, recognize that a smaller ad will have a hard time competing.

Rather than packing lots of information into your ad, focus on one key benefit you provide or one problem you solve for your clients. On a page filled with ads for psychotherapy that mention depression, relationship problems, and eating disorders, an ad highlighting "recovery from trauma" will instantly attract someone suffering from posttraumatic stress disorder. If you can't decide which of your services to promote, pick the one no one else is advertising. Remember that the sole purpose of an ad like this is to make your phone ring.

And beware of new, untested directories. Just because a distributor prints 50,000 copies doesn't mean anyone will be using them.

## Print Advertising

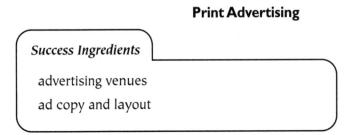

*Success Ingredients*

advertising venues

ad copy and layout

The variety of *advertising venues* in print is truly enormous. You can place display, classified, or calendar listing ads in newspapers, magazines, newsletters, trade journals, or event programs. How do you choose? This is where targeting is extremely important. There's no point in placing an ad in a publication your target market doesn't read. You also may find that periodicals with a large circulation are far too expensive for you to consider, while specialized publications aimed only at your market are more affordable.

Look for venues where you could be the only advertiser in your category, or offer something completely unique. A career counselor might get a good response from a small classified above the "Help Wanted" section that read, "Looking for something different? I can help you find meaningful work. Call for a free newsletter."

Use the services of a graphic designer, copywriter, or marketing communications professional to make sure your *ad copy and layout* will attract attention. Just as in directory advertising, narrow the focus of your ad to one key point that will resonate with your best prospective customers.

The headline of your ad is the most important part of its design. If the headline doesn't attract attention, your ad won't be read. Inexperienced advertisers often make the mistake of headlining their ad with the name of their company. But no one cares who your company is unless they need what you have to offer.

Effective headlines directly address a prospect's needs by stating a principal benefit of the service being offered, or mentioning a problem the prospect may have. Here are some examples:

> We Buy Business Invoices for Cash
> Does Your Computer Give You a Pain in the Neck?
> Affordable Bankruptcy
> How Safe Are Your Investments?
> Adults With Attention Deficit Disorder
> Health Insurance at a Price That Won't Make You Sick
> Relationship Troubles?

Remember to track the results of every ad you run carefully. It's the only way you will know what works and what doesn't.

### Advertising on the Web

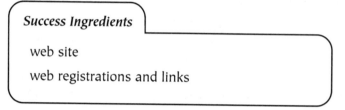

*Success Ingredients*

web site

web registrations and links

The basic tool for advertising via the Internet is a *web site,* an address on the World Wide Web where you display one or many pages of information about your services. The best sites are those that go beyond being electronic versions of your brochure. Instead, they provide much useful information to your prospective clients. You can post informative articles, lists of Frequently Asked Questions (FAQs), and links to other sites that might be of interest to your visitors.

The more of a resource your site is, the more often your clients and prospects will visit. Updating the information on your site frequently will encourage repeat visits. Interactive features like bulletin boards or live chats will also stimulate more traffic.

Actively maintaining a site with many features can be a huge undertaking. If you are a one-person business, the amount of time and money involved in doing this may not be worthwhile. A simple, well-designed site that gives some basic information may be all the web presence you need. Remember to ask yourself the essential question about any advertising medium: Is there a cheaper way you could generate the same amount of revenue?

Hiring a professional web designer to build your site will save you a great deal of frustration. Be sure to ask about the range of the designer's expertise. If you are working with someone whose skills are mainly artistic or technical, you may also want to consider getting additional help from a marketing professional.

Once you have a site, you can point prospective clients there by putting its address on your business card, marketing literature, and voice-mail message, and listing it in any print ads. To attract new prospects to it, you will need *web registrations and links* for people to find you. Registering your site with as many search engines as possible is one way to get people to visit. Doing a keyword search of the web for "search engine submission" will tell you more about this process than you ever wanted to know, as well as direct you to innumerable companies that will perform this task for you.

Another strategy for attracting people to your site is to ask related sites if they will post a link to you. Many will do this for free if they see your site as a useful resource to their visitors, or if you offer to post a link to their site in return. Others may wish to charge you a fee for listing your site in their on-line mall, or displaying a banner ad on their site that links directly to yours when visitors click on it.

Before you start building a web page, spend some time surfing. Search for keywords you think your prospective clients would use to find you, and see what else is out there. Be sure to check out the sites of your competitors. Keep a list of features you like and dislike, as well as what you think the competitive advantages of your site should be. And don't spend more on your site than you think it will bring you in added business.

---

"The biggest mistake people make in marketing themselves on the Internet is believing that if you build a great-looking web site, people will flock to visit," says Margo Komenar, the author of *Electronic Marketing* (Wiley, 1997). Margo finds that most entrepreneurs spend far more money on their site than is necessary or appropriate. Then they fail to design an equally great marketing and positioning strategy.

Margo suggests that before you design your site, make an overall plan for promoting your business, which will include getting the word out about your site. In her booklet, *Marketing on the Net Made Easy*, Margo recommends these key strategies to promote your site and gain visibility on the Net:

1. Contact other qualified sites that you can create mutual links with or contribute content to. Don't do this just once; continue to contact new sites on a regular basis.

2. Visit sites on topics related to your own, and notice who their content and advertising partners are. You can get lots of great ideas from your competitors.

3. Find newsletters on the net that are e-mailed to your target audience, and offer to contribute.

4. Visit chat groups regularly, and become a familiar contributor and topic expert.

5. Find a listserve to participate in and offer your advice whenever possible. Spend some time "lurking" first; then join in with a mix of your own inquiries and expert advice.

Margo Komenar, M.A., business coach and
marketing consultant, www.komenar.com

## Radio and TV Advertising

> *Success Ingredients*
>
> advertising venues
>
> ad script

Can you afford to advertise in the broadcast media? Maybe. Is it the best place to spend your advertising dollars? Maybe not. Yes, broadcast advertising can bring you name recognition with a wide audience. But is there a cheaper way to get the same result?

Go back and reread the introduction to this section, and see if this medium is really worth pursuing. Watch or listen to the stations you might consider as *advertising venues*. Are there any other businesses like yours advertised? If not, there might be a reason.

Especially in radio and television, repeat advertising is the name of the game. Your prospective clients can't tear out your ad and save it, so unless your ad runs constantly, they need to be interested enough at the moment they hear it to write down your phone number or remember your name. It's a pretty long shot.

One of the few valid reasons for a small service business to use broadcast advertising is if your average sale is so low that you need many, many prospects calling you. In this situation, you might find it necessary to spend more on advertising to get the phone to ring. But be sure to do your math first. No business is profitable unless it earns more per customer than it costs to get each one in the door.

To produce an effective radio or TV ad, professional help with your *ad script* and production is mandatory. There's no point in spending big bucks to air a second-rate ad. If the station you plan to advertise with offers to produce your ad for you, survey the quality of other ads it has produced and make sure they meet your standards. As with all other media, track the results of your ads carefully. If you're not getting the results you want, pull the plug.

# Chapter 8

# Following Up:
# When You Have Plenty of
# Numbers But You're Not Calling

*You must do the thing you think you cannot do.*

—Eleanor Roosevelt

### It's Simple, But Not Always Easy

Doing a good job at follow-up is a piece of cake. You just capture every lead or potential referral partner you run across, then place a call or send them something, or both. If you don't make a sale right away, you put them on the calendar for the next follow-up and do the same thing again. Pretty straightforward, isn't it? So why is follow-up such a problem? Here are the four most common reasons:

1. *Prioritization.* With an activity that you must initiate, it's easy to let other tasks come first: responding to incoming calls and mail, getting the invoices out, going to networking events, and, oh yes, doing the client work you get paid for. If you don't set aside reserved time for follow-up, it will never happen.

2. *Disorganization.* Business cards and scraps of paper lying on your desk do not constitute a contact management system. Without accurate records of the people you have contacted, when, and what your last conversation was about, effective follow-up is impossible.

3. *Resistance.* Do you find yourself saying, "Why do I have to do this? I'm good at what I do. Why aren't the prospects calling me?" You are sabotaging yourself with this line of thinking. Business owners much more established than you are do follow-up every day. It's one of the ways they got established. Regular follow-up does not make peo-

ple think you don't have enough business; it makes them see you as a professional.

4. *Fear.* "If I follow up that lead, I might be rejected," reasons the voice in your head. "So I'll avoid the pain by not making the call in the first place." Or conversely, you may be thinking, "If I place the call, I might get the business, and then I'll have to do the work, and people will have all these expectations of me." The reality is that if you don't place the calls, you're going to fail even more dramatically than in these two imaginary scenarios.

By using the Get Clients Now! system to begin with, you are already addressing three of these issues. The 28-day program will help you to set better priorities, as well as to overcome resistance and break through fear. So let's tackle disorganization next.

## Managing Your Contacts

*Success Ingredients*

contact management system

computer

Having some kind of *contact management system* is absolutely essential to efficient follow-up. Your chosen method for keeping track of contacts could be a box of 3- by 5-inch cards, a rotary card file, a three-ring binder, or a computer system (usually with some information on paper as well). In addition to name, address, phone, fax, and e-mail, you should also note the source of each contact and when you were first in touch.

Each time you follow up with a contact, or he or she follows up with you, make a note of when it was, what happened, and when you plan to follow up next. With a computer-based system, once you enter the next follow-up date, you can run a report or use a "tickler" feature to see when it's due. If your system is paper based, you should put the next follow-up date in your calendar so you don't forget about it.

Once you are managing more than 300 contacts, a *computer* really becomes necessary. A computer-based contact management system will allow you to sort and select contacts by location, original source, date of last contact, or other helpful information. You can use it to print labels, create an e-mail list, or merge personalized information into a boilerplate letter. Other reasons to use a computer in marketing include being able to revise letters and other marketing literature easily, send and receive e-mail, and surf the Net.

Many prefer to use software specifically designed for contact management, such as ACT!, Now Contact, or GoldMine. However, if you are already familiar with a generic database tool, such as FileMaker Pro, you may find it simpler to use what you have than to learn something new. Don't try to use a word processing or spreadsheet program as a contact manager, though. They don't have the range of capabilities you need.

---

Shannon Seek is a personal and professional coach and professional organizer who specializes in working with super-achievers. "Keeping your contacts and prospects organized," Shannon points out, "is the only way you can expect to be effective at follow-up. You need a designated place to keep contact information until you act on it, a system for organizing the information, and a system for tracking what you do with it.

"When you first meet someone, make a note on the person's business card of when and where you met, and what action you intend to take. Keep all the cards or other notes like this in one place until you make the call, send the letter, or whatever else you do. Then file the person so you can find him again, by either name or company. If you use a computer-based contact manager, enter the person now and make updates every time you contact him.

"You should categorize your contacts as much as possible. With a computerized system, you can have multiple categories. Think about grouping them by:

"• The product or service they are most interested in

"• Their level of interest (hot, warm, or cold)

"• When you want to contact them next (two weeks, one month, six months)

"• Their industry or field

"• Significant affiliations (e.g., Chamber of Commerce or trade association)

"• Geographical region

"It may take some work to set up your tracking system at the beginning, but it's worth the effort. If you make your system easy to work with and convenient to access, you will remember to use it."

Shannon Seek, Certified Professional and Personal Coach,
www.SeekSolutions.com

## Global Follow-Up Tools

*Success Ingredients*

brochure              30-second commercial

marketing kit

## Brochure

The first thing you should consider about creating a brochure is whether you need one at all. Many successful consultants and professionals never develop a brochure, relying instead on personal letters and a few supplements, such as a professional biography or résumé and a client list. When you are just starting out, paying for the design and printing of a brochure can be an expensive mistake if the nature of your services, or profile of your target market, is still in flux.

Look at what your competitors are doing. If they all seem to have brochures, you probably need one also. If they don't, or there seem to be mixed opinions on the subject in your field, ask yourself whether having a brochure will make a positive difference with your prospective clients. If you think it will, how much brochure can you afford?

The simplest and most inexpensive brochure is a standard trifold that you or a desktop publisher lays out, and prints or photocopies on preprinted brochure paper. For marketing personal or household services to individuals, this may be all you need. For business-to-business marketing, a professionally designed and printed brochure will be much more effective. As a general rule, the more expensive your service is, the more expensive your marketing materials should be. Hire a graphic designer, copywriter, or marketing communications specialist to help you, and be sure to work out a budget in advance.

The best way to decide what will go into your brochure is to review many examples of what others have included.

### Typical Elements of a Trifold Brochure

- Attention-getting cover design, perhaps with a logo
- List of the services you offer
- Benefits and features of your services
- Brief biography of you, your company, or both
- Client list, testimonials, or quotes
- Photographs or illustrations of you or the work you do
- Address, phone, fax, e-mail, and web site

## Marketing Kit

When marketing to businesses and organizations, a marketing kit is more common than a brochure. A typical kit begins with a two-pocket 8½- by 11-inch folder with a cut-out to hold your business card. The contents of your kit are similar to the elements of a trifold brochure, with each item laid out on a separate page. Other ingredients might be:

- Articles written by you, about you, or about the kind of work you do
- Testimonial letters from clients
- Case study of a successful project
- Actual samples of work you have produced

A significant advantage of using a kit like this is that you can customize its contents for each recipient. Because you are assembling kits only as you need them, this can be much more affordable than printing several hundred brochures. You can also easily update individual sheets.

Don't overload clients with information, especially on the first contact. Hold back some of what you have, and use it in further follow-up, or as leave-behinds after a presentation.

## 30-Second Commercial

When you are calling someone for the first time and get voice mail, use a 30-second commercial to introduce yourself. You may or may not get a return call, but it is a golden opportunity to deliver your marketing message directly into a prospect's ear. A 30-second commercial is also useful in networking groups or other situations where you have a chance to let a gathering of interested people know more about what you do.

Begin your commercial with your 10-second introduction (see Chapter 7); then continue on with a few details about the services you offer. Try to include benefits or results to the client rather than just a list of what you provide. Here's an example:

> My name is Susan Schwartz, and I help real people get dressed. My business is U: A Personal Design Service. I'm a personal style consultant. I work with colors, closets, clothes, and classes. I help you define and refine your personal style, so you can have a working wardrobe that works for you 100 percent of the time. I'll create a personalized color palette for you, help you clear out your closet, show you what works for you—and why—and take you shopping. Can you afford me? If you have even one outfit in

your closet that you don't wear, you've more than paid for my services. If you're tired of fighting the wardrobe wars, call me.

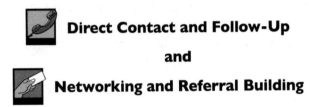

## Direct Contact and Follow-Up

## and

## Networking and Referral Building

In the follow-up stage of marketing, you are using only two strategies: direct contact and follow-up, and networking and referral building. It's important to notice that the activities involved in pursuing these strategies are identical: calling and mailing, follow-up meetings, follow-up mailings, and electronic follow-up. The difference is in the target of these activities. Direct contact and follow-up is aimed at prospects, and networking and referral building can be aimed at either prospects or referral partners.

In professions where directly soliciting business is inappropriate, you may be using the strategies in this chapter more for networking to increase referrals than for making contact with prospects. Nevertheless, don't neglect to follow up with prospects as much as you can without crossing the line. Sending a nice-to-meet-you note, interesting article, or informational newsletter is appropriate for any business.

### Calling and Mailing

> **Success Ingredient**
>
> model marketing letters

When you are contacting someone for the first time, whether it is a potential customer or a possible referral partner, the most effective approach is to call, mail, and call. In other words, call before you mail, and call again after you mail. Your first call is to find out if you are talking to the right person, and if you reach him or her, gauging the interest level in what you have to offer. If you find you are talking to someone both interested and qualified (for example, able to pay), you may be able to arrange a presentation or a networking meeting on your first call. There's more information about this in Chapter 7.

According to Ellen Looyen of Magnetic Marketing, "In a successful marketing piece, everything works together to support the marketing position and message. The copywriting should be persuasive, and the design compelling." By helping thousands of businesspeople—entrepreneurs and professionals—to position and package their businesses, Ellen has discovered that "an effective brochure needs to exude confidence and convey a sense of quality, honesty, and knowledge to your prospects. It also needs to be written in your prospect's language; generic language is not very effective in the relational marketplace.

"Tell your prospects what you do, how you do it, and who can benefit from what you're offering. It works best to bullet point as much of this information as possible, so readers can scan for what interests them, instead of having to read every word. Be sure to include a list of several tangible benefits your clients will receive. The most important information in a brochure answers the question, 'What's in it for the client?'

"Endorsements and testimonials work well, because people tend to do what their peers do. Be sure your testimonials point to specific results and are not just fluff. If you can get a testimonial from a well-respected expert in your field, highlight it in a shaded box, so it gets the notice it deserves.

"Include a biography that instills confidence in your prospects and positions you as an expert in your field. Tell readers what motivated you to get into this business, and why you are the ideal person to be doing this. Highlight your education, credentials, and accomplishments. Give a success story that illustrates the benefits you have achieved for other clients. Make your brochure convey your uniqueness and value with passion and believability."

Ellen Looyen, marketing consultant, Magnetic Marketing,
www.el-magnetic-mktg.com

It's more likely, though, you will reach voice mail, an assistant, or someone with "no time to talk." This is why being organized and persistent about follow-up is so important. Once you have made an initial contact, even if only through voice mail or a receptionist, you must follow up with a mailing, another call, a fax or e-mail, or even stopping by—and you will probably have to do this more than once.

Never assume that someone you are calling is going to call you back. Usually they won't. Busy people simply don't have the time to return unsolicited phone calls or, in fact, any call that isn't their top priority that day. If you are of the opinion that not returning a phone call is rude, get over it. Even people you are in the final stages of negotiating a contract with will often not return calls for days or weeks. If you are willing to accept this as a normal business practice, your marketing life will be much less stressful.

When sending mail to someone you have not yet spoken to, keep it simple. Until you know whether the person is interested, don't send more than a personal letter with a brochure or fact sheet enclosed. On the other hand, if an initial conversation prompted interest but not an appointment for a meeting or discussion, you may wish to send more information in the hope of convincing him to meet with you. If you use a marketing kit, this is typically when you would send it.

To make this process easier, it is helpful to have several model *marketing letters*, standard letters that you can personalize to fit a specific situation. Your first paragraph typically introduces you or your company. When writing to a prospect, lead off with an attention-getting sentence, such as, "Would you like to increase sales by 30 percent this year?" or "Learn to lose weight, stay fit, and extend your life in less than 30 minutes a day!"

In your second paragraph, highlight the benefits of what you offer. Don't just repeat what is in your brochure; expand on it or talk about some actual client results. Use the third paragraph to suggest how you can help the prospect you are writing to. Only the third paragraph needs to be personalized.

You might have a model letter for each different service you offer, one for each target market, or one for prospects and another for referral partners. Unless you are using a letter to completely replace a brochure, one page is all you need. See Figure 8-1 for an example.

A week to ten days after sending your information, place a follow-up call. Never assume that if your prospects were interested, they would call. Think about how many days or weeks a low-priority task can languish on your own to-do list. When you get a prospect on the phone, try again for a presentation. If it doesn't happen this time either, ask if you can follow up at some later date, and determine what an appropriate interval would be: next month, next quarter, or even next year. Then make the entry in your contact management system and move on to the next prospect.

What if you keep getting voice mail? While it is true that some people leave their voice mail on all the time, you can sometimes get through by call-

**Figure 8-1. Sample marketing letter.**

Rebecca DuBois
Human Resources Director
Lone Star Telecom
555 Amarillo Street
Houston, TX 77057

Dear Rebecca:

Is your human resources system meeting your needs? Can your current system handle all your specialized requirements? If you think it might be time to upgrade or replace your HR system, Winston HR Solutions can help. We specialize in assisting clients with the most complex HR systems applications: compensation, health and welfare plans, retirement plans, and payroll interfaces. Our services include needs analysis, system installation, data conversion, and software customization.

Our staff of experienced consultants can help you:

- Avoid expensive mistakes in software selection and implementation

- Increase system response time and accuracy

- Satisfy the newest government regulations

- Improve capability and efficiency without replacing your current system

With the rapid growth that Lone Star Telecom is experiencing, you need a system that can respond to increased hiring, policy changes, and new incentive plans quickly and efficiently. Winston HR Solutions can make sure you have that system. I look forward to speaking with you soon.

Sincerely,

Christopher J. Winston
Senior Consultant

ing off hours, say before 8:30 or after 5:30. You may also find people at their desks during lunch hour. But should you keep calling or leave a message? Actually, you should do both. Since you are assuming that most people won't call you back, keep right on calling them.

Whether you reach your contacts or not, never make them wrong for not returning your calls. Rather than saying (no doubt somewhat peevishly), "I haven't heard from you," let them know you are eager to speak with them and wanted to try again while you were in your office. As a general rule, leaving three voice-mail messages over a ten-day period of time is sufficient. If you get no response, wait a month and try again.

When you do leave a message, use your 30-second commercial on the first call. In later messages, leave a new and interesting piece of information each time. When calling a prospect, make it a benefit of doing business with you—for example, "I can help you save up to 20 percent on your contract labor costs." Keep your voice-mail messages to no more than 30 seconds; no one likes to receive long voice mails from strangers, and the delete key is at their fingertips.

If you have called, left messages, and still can't get through to the person you want, send an e-mail. Many people will quickly respond to e-mail because it is easy. If you can interest them in what you have to offer (without revealing all the details), they may be willing to set up a phone appointment with you to find out more. If you don't have the person's e-mail address, try doing the same thing by fax.

Whether you should ever stop calling depends on the value of the potential sale. A $1,000 sale might be worth only two or three calls to you, but a $10,000 sale would certainly pay for many more. Every salesperson has a story about a customer who finally said yes after the seventeenth phone call, so if it seems worth it, don't quit.

## Follow-Up Meetings

Your first in-person meeting with a prospect is typically some sort of presentation. Even if it is primarily a fact-finding meeting, you will be spending some time talking about your services and qualifications. If a second meeting is necessary, it might be a formal presentation to a larger group, an informal meeting when you present a proposal you have prepared, or a discussion about the details of the proposed work. After this, you may find yourself following up mostly by phone, e-mail, letter, or fax.

The same is also true for referral partners. After an initial meeting (which could even be by phone), you might not see them again in person. When following up over a long period of time, try to find ways to meet with your contacts or prospects face to face again to keep the relationship alive. Take them to lunch, meet for coffee or a drink, stop by their offices (if this would be acceptable), or seek them out at networking events.

## Follow-Up Mailings

*Success Ingredients*

personal mailing list    newsletter

postcard or mailer

Whenever you meet someone at a networking event who is not an immediate prospect, an easy and inexpensive way to follow up immediately is to send a nice-to-meet-you note. Depending on the nature of the contact, you might include an interesting article or even your brochure. Then add the person to your contact management system for later follow-up.

As you work to fill the pipeline, you will constantly be collecting names and addresses for your *personal mailing list*. If you enter the ones you want to keep into your contact management system as you collect them, eventually you will have a substantial list. When your list reaches about 300 names, it's probably time to start thinking about some kind of mailer to send on a regular basis. We are talking here about follow-up mail to people you already know, not direct mail sent to strangers on a prospect list you bought or compiled.

As a rule, sending a general mailing four times per year is sufficient to keep your name visible to your prospects and referral partners. With hot prospects or frequent referrers, you will probably want to be in contact more often. In addition to phone calls or meetings, you might send these people personal notes, along with articles of interest, amusing cartoons, or invitations to upcoming events.

For your general mailing, you could opt for a simple piece like a *postcard or mailer*, or put the effort into publishing your own *newsletter*. Postcards, self-mailers, and other small pieces typically take the form of reminders or seasonal announcements with an attention-getting tag line and graphic. Here are some examples:

> *Overloaded with year-end work? Time to call Professional Solutions.*
> *Sales in a slump? Take Charge Marketing can help.*
> *January special—25% off your first appointment!*

Keep the amount of text to a minimum. A mailer is not intended to do the job of a brochure. What you want is for the recipients to call you with their questions, not get all the information they need from your mailer.

Producing a newsletter can be a sizable job, requiring skills on several levels: how-to writing for articles, copywriting for promotional sections, and graphic design for art and layout. Unless you are a professional in these areas, get help from someone who is. Homemade newsletters usually look it, and there's no point putting in this much time and money if your prospects won't be impressed.

A promotional newsletter can be as few as two pages or as many as eight. If you decide to produce a fax newsletter rather than print and mail it, you may only have one page. Be sure your newsletter contains a balance of useful information and promotional copy. Ideally, you want the people on your mailing list not only to read your newsletter but to pass it along to friends.

## Electronic Follow-Up

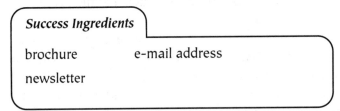

*Success Ingredients*

brochure          e-mail address

newsletter

Having an e-mail *newsletter* is becoming more and more popular. Since it doesn't have to be printed and typically involves no design work, the time and expense to produce one are minimal compared to a print version. If a significant portion of your mailing list has e-mail addresses, you may want to consider this option.

Be aware, however, that on-line culture has different conventions from communicating by mail. Unsolicited e-mail annoys many recipients and may get you a nasty message—and bad feelings—in response. When you send out your e-mail newsletter for the first time, label it "Complimentary Issue," and ask people to respond if they don't want to receive another. If someone asks to be removed from the distribution list, be sure to honor the request.

With e-mail newsletters being cheap and easy, it may be tempting to send one more often. Monthly promotional newsletters are not uncommon, and some are weekly or even daily (although these last are usually quite short). Weigh your time commitment against the expected return before you commit to a frequent schedule. A monthly newsletter may not get you any more results than a bimonthly or quarterly one.

Once you have an *e-mail address*, you may find many other types of follow-up possible through this medium. For clients who like to communicate this way, knowing your e-mail address is essential, so print it on all your literature. Try e-mailing people who don't return your phone calls, but remember to keep it personal; don't send an advertisement this way.

"FEAR stands for False Evidence Appearing Real. Our fear is an emotional expression of nonempowering beliefs, which are falsely evidenced by stories from our past. These beliefs appear real, because we keep reinforcing them within ourselves. What are the emotions that come up for you when you try to market yourself? Self-doubt? Fear of rejection? Lack of confidence? What are the nonempowering beliefs you hold that feed these emotions?

"An example might be, 'If I try to sell myself, I will be rejected.' Question this belief. Try asking yourself what you would need to believe instead, in order to sell your services successfully. For example: 'If I try to sell myself, some people will buy from me.' Looking at other possible beliefs you could hold will begin to break down the nonempowering ones."

Barry Bettman, business and personal coach,
Get Results Now, www.barrybettman.com

You may find it convenient to have an e-mail version of your *brochure*. This is typically just the text of your brochure laid out to appear attractively in a mail reading window, which you paste directly into a message you are sending. More sophisticated methods are available, but not all recipients will be able to view other formats or willing to download alien files. Again, don't e-mail your brochure to a stranger. Use it to respond to an inquiry or follow up with someone who has already expressed interest.

## Another Word About Fear

The thought of making follow-up calls may be even more paralyzing than cold calling. After all, this is someone you already believe needs your services. Maybe you've already talked or sent your literature. You've invested something or made a personal connection, so now if you hear no, the rejection really feels personal.

What you have to remember is that rejection is not about you. This is a business transaction. Your prospect is deciding whether to spend her own or the company's money. The number of factors that go into a decision like this are innumerable. Here are some actual reasons people with a strong need for the service being offered have refused to buy or have bought from a competitor:

- Decided to take a Hawaiian vacation instead
- Competing bid was from cousin's boyfriend

- Getting divorced
- Company going bankrupt
- Didn't want to take money out of a mutual fund to pay for it
- Boss doesn't want headquarters to know there's a problem
- Liked the competitor's logo
- Project was tabled until next year

When a prospect tells you a competitor was chosen because he or she "has more experience," the message is that the company hires only people with strong experience in its own industry. This is not about you. If you are told the competition "came well recommended," the prospect is choosing to do business with the friend of a colleague. It's not about you. When you hear that the other guy's bid was lower, it means the buyer values price over quality. Also, not about you.

The real trick to vanquishing fear of follow-up is to have so many prospects in the pipeline that any one no becomes much less important.

# Chapter 9

# Getting Presentations: When You're Making (or Taking) Calls But Not Getting Appointments

*Consider the postage stamp. . . . It secures success through its ability to stick to one thing until it gets there.*

—Josh Billings, nineteenth-century Yankee humorist

## What's in the Way?

If you've gotten to this stage in the universal marketing cycle, you are more than halfway home. With a full pipeline and consistent follow-up, you are bound to make plenty of sales, right? Well, usually that's true. Finding the right people to talk to, and actually talking to them, will produce results in most cases. But sometimes it's not quite enough.

When you find yourself making lots of contacts but rarely getting to the presentation (whether that's in person or on the phone), there's something in the way. Assuming that you have a service that your target market needs and it's priced within the range your market can pay, what else might be preventing people from wanting to hear what you have to offer?

### Barriers to Getting Presentations

1. You're not using the right words. When you send a letter or call on the phone, or prospects call you, they aren't understanding how you can help them.

2. Your telemarketing skills aren't up to the task. You are nervous or unprepared when you get on the phone, and aren't able to engage people in conversation.

3. The prospects you are talking to aren't qualified enough. They don't have a need, can't pay, or are otherwise not ready to take action.

4. You aren't well known enough, or haven't been recommended, so prospects are hesitant to take their time to talk with you.

5. Your competition seems to have the market locked up. No one wants to talk to you because they're already being served by someone else.

6. You are offering your prospects what you think they need instead of what they think they need. They don't see how your service fits into their plans.

7. The way your services are packaged doesn't make sense to your prospects. For example, they want to pay a flat fee, and you are charging by the hour.

8. You are offering so many services that your prospects can't quite figure out what you actually do and how it matches up with their needs.

In the next two sections, you will find solutions to many of these problems. Suggestions for doing a better job at making contact with your prospects appear first, followed by some ideas for improving your strategic market position.

 **Direct Contact and Follow-Up**

### Making the Pitch

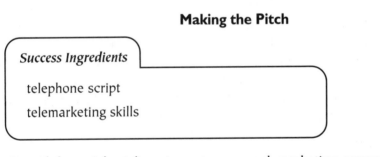

*Success Ingredients*

telephone script

telemarketing skills

One of the quickest fixes to your personal marketing approach can be to change the words you use. An effective *telephone script* positions what you are offering in such a way that prospects grasp what's in it for them. A common mistake is to call prospects with the intent of introducing yourself and telling them what you do. But that's about you. Why should they care?

Instead, after a brief introduction, ask about them. "Do you have a moment to talk about your concerns with system response time?" is a sample

"Most up-front objections are avoidance tactics," claims author Tony Alessandra. "The prospect doesn't want to talk to you because he's afraid you're going to pressure him, so he hits you with objections that he hopes are difficult to counter. But if you have done a good job targeting your prospects, you know there's a good chance your service will interest him.

"Open with your competitive advantage statement, including a specific benefit for this customer. When the prospect says he has no need, let him know you won't try to sell him anything unless you can show how you can help him: increase profits, decrease costs, or increase productivity. Tell him the purpose of your call is to begin building a mutually beneficial relationship and learn enough about his company to be specific about the benefits he'll receive.

"If your prospect is too busy or has no time to see you now, ask to schedule an appointment at a more convenient time, or ask for a phone interview. Promise not to take up any more time than he'll allow you. Stress that you really do want to get to know him and his business a little better and that you're willing to go out of your way to do it.

"What if your prospect has no time to see you at all? You might say that's exactly why he should take the time to see you—if you sell a product or service that is more convenient, can save time, or free him of something he currently has to do himself, such as financial planning or recruiting new employees.

"When you come across a prospect who's happy with her current supplier, you might ask, 'Of all the things you like about your present supplier, what one thing do you wish he could do better?' Look for areas where you have a competitive uniqueness or advantage. Help the prospect discover for herself some discontent with her existing supplier."

Tony Alessandra, Ph.D., speaker and author,
www.alessandra.com

opening question. Try leading with a benefit: "I help companies increase employee retention without added costs. Is employee turnover a problem you're concerned about?" Or ask a qualifying question as your first step: "Are you experiencing a slump or plateau in sales?"

This is also what you should do when prospects call you. Before launching into a description of how you work and what it costs, ask about their situation.

Engaging your prospects in conversation will both establish rapport and provide you with valuable information. Whenever you can, ask open-ended questions rather than encouraging yes or no answers. "How much use do you expect to make of outside trainers this year?" can get you much more information than asking, "Does your company use outside trainers?" Include a series of possible questions like this in your script.

The word *script* is not meant to imply that you are reading something prepared. You don't want to come off as if you are selling newspaper subscriptions. Design your script as a list of talking points that you refer to as needed during an interactive conversation.

When you feel that you have both established rapport and collected enough information from your prospects, tell them briefly and specifically how you can help them, and in their words. If the prospect says, "Our employee turnover is out of control," you might respond with, "I can really help you with that out-of-control turnover situation. The incentive plan I implemented for Althea Chemical reduced their turnover by 20 percent."

As soon as you know you've got the person's interest, ask for a meeting or launch into your phone presentation. Don't wait for her to suggest the next step or back away from making it a direct question. "It sounds as if my services might be just what you're looking for. Would you like to get together and talk about it?" Expect to encounter objections, and have a ready answer for each predictable stumbling block already in your script.

If you have trouble remembering what's in your script, get nervous once you're on the phone, or just can't seem to think quickly enough to deliver the right responses, you need to work on your *telemarketing skills*. Take a class, listen to a tape, or practice with friends. Learning your script more thoroughly will enable you to give a better performance under stress.

## Qualifying Your Prospects

*Success Ingredients*

qualifying questions

higher-quality leads and referrals

One of the barriers to landing presentations is pursuing the wrong prospects. You may have done a good job at defining your target market, but not everyone in your market needs you or can afford to pay. *Qualifying questions* are intended to determine whether a prospect is hot, warm, or cold, so you can gauge your level of effort accordingly.

Consulting firm chairman Nido Qubein maintains that targeting is the solution to more than just finding the right market. In his book *How to Sell Professional Services* (New Ventures, 1998), Nido shares some other ways to use targeting to get prospects to respond:

1. *Target the prospective client.* People will give you what you want if you show them how to get what they want through using your services. What's in it for the client?

2. *Target the key issue.* As you ask questions, usually one major concern or issue will surface above all the rest. Let that be the primary focus of your entire approach.

3. *Target the hot button.* What does your prospect like about your service? How does he or she perceive the benefits to be obtained from it? Make this your strongest point. When major advertisers have only 30 seconds to deliver a message, a great deal of work goes into their Unique Selling Proposition. The less time you have, the more effective yours must be.

4. *Target your timing.* Study the monologue of a well-known comedian the next time you see one. Notice the timing of words and phrases for maximum effect. Know that the prospect's time is valuable, and get to the point as soon as rapport is established. Remember, the writer of Genesis told the whole creation story in 434 words.

5. *Target your answers.* Answer every question your prospect asks. Respond to direct questions with direct answers. If you don't know, say so. Evasiveness will come back to haunt you when it's time to wrap up the order.

6. *Target your facts.* Sometimes we get so excited about our services that we tend to exaggerate the benefits. Don't promise what you can't deliver!

Nido Qubein, Chairman, Creative Services

*Typical Qualifying Questions*

- Asking if they have a particular problem your service solves or an opportunity it aids

- Finding out how much they are expecting to pay or have paid in the past

- Determining if they have a budget set aside for the work

- Asking how soon they are expecting to get started or have the project completed

- Knowing if the person you are talking to is the decision maker

If you find that once you start asking these questions, your prospect list starts looking pretty chilly, you need some *higher-quality leads and referrals.* What is the profile of the customer most likely to buy? Where can you get more leads that fit that profile? If you don't know the answers to these questions, you may need to do more research on your target market. (See the next section for some suggestions.)

Another solution is getting more referral-based leads, rather than working from prospect lists or relying on networking contacts. A customer who is referred to you will almost always move forward to the presentation stage immediately, because they have prequalified *you.*

**Networking and Referral Building**

**and**

**Public Speaking**

**and**

**Writing and Publicity**

*Success Ingredient*

professional visibility

If the first time that prospective clients hear your name is when you call them to make an appointment, you will find it much harder to get their attention than if they already know you or know of you. Increasing your *professional visibility* is not just a tactic for filling the pipeline; it's also a way to influence buying decisions.

Consider using networking and referral building to start becoming more visible. Attend networking events frequented by your clients. Volunteer in a high-profile position, such as the program committee of an association your clients belong to, or a project likely to get good coverage in the trade press. The strategies of writing and publicity and public speaking will also help you to become more visible professionally, while simultaneously building your credibility.

## Evaluating Your Market Position

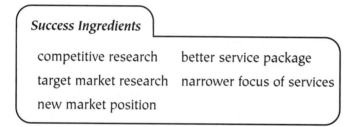

*Success Ingredients*

competitive research      better service package

target market research    narrower focus of services

new market position

The position that you occupy in the minds of your prospective clients can be a critical factor in their decision to meet with you or not. If you find that prospects are choosing to work with your competitors, you may need to reposition yourself against the competition. Try conducting some *competitive research* to find out what it is that clients like about the people you are competing with. Are those qualities you can emulate? In what areas are clients not as satisfied with them? Could you offer them more satisfaction there?

Start by asking your current or former clients about their experience with the competition. They may be quite candid with you about what they liked and didn't like, and also give you some valuable insight into why they chose you. To expand your research to prospective clients, you could approach them directly with your questions, but many won't want to answer. Consider hiring a market researcher to survey them for you. They may be much more willing to speak with a third party.

An easy way to check out how your competitors are positioning themselves without revealing what you're up to is surfing the Net. Mission statements, lists of features and benefits, and other valuable information will often be posted on their web sites. You can also have a friend request their literature or hire a researcher to help.

*Target market research* may be another direction to look if prospects are telling you they don't need what you are offering. If you think they need a team-building retreat, but they think their problem can be solved with more skills training, you won't make a sale. When you learn more about how prospects view their own challenges, you can develop a *new market position* to match their mental, or real-life, purchase order better. Your retreat just might fly if you called it "an intensive three-day training program in the critical skills needed for effective teamwork."

Don't forget to ask current and former clients to help you position your services correctly. One way to discover how your market perceives the value in your work is to ask satisfied clients for a testimonial letter. The way they describe the work you do and benefits they received from it can give you valuable clues in how to sell it to others. An evaluation questionnaire can be used for the same purpose. Try asking, "How would you describe my service to someone else who could use it?"

It's also possible you will discover that you've chosen the wrong market; the perceived need for what you offer just isn't strong enough, they aren't willing to pay what you need to charge, or the size of the market is too small. In this case, it's time to position yourself for an entirely different market. Make sure you do your homework on any possible new markets in advance, so you won't make the same mistake a second time.

A career counselor who is having a hard time finding individuals who will pay her fee can market herself to companies in need of outplacement services. A computer software trainer who discovers that large companies prefer working with training firms that can serve them on a national scale might find a better market in small to midsize organizations. Keep asking the question, "Who is most likely to hire me?" until you find the right fit.

Another problem your research might uncover is that your service isn't packaged in a way that prospects want to buy it. Developing a *better service package* could make what you offer more attractive. A marketing consultant who has been working on a project basis might find clients more receptive to a monthly retainer they can budget for. An interior designer encountering resistance to paying an hourly fee might instead raise his commission rate on furnishings, and no longer charge by the hour.

Sometimes just naming your service package can make a difference. An image consultant might be much more successful selling the "one-day makeover" than suggesting to clients they buy six hours of her time to revamp their whole look. When doing your market research, try asking your prospects how they prefer to buy services like yours, and tailor your offering to their preferences.

One final roadblock you may be putting in your own way is offering too much. When someone asks exactly what it is that you do or specifically how you can help them, it really doesn't work to say, "I can do pretty much anything in the area of [fill in the blank]. What do you need?" It may be absolutely

"All the tips and tricks in the world don't work unless a business has a good service or product for which there is a market," according to Allison Bliss, a consultant who specializes in helping companies expand their market potential. "The number one reason businesses fail is that business owners don't determine whether there is a market for their products or services before they launch their business. Therefore, accurate market research is a key to successfully introducing, defining, positioning, packaging, and promoting your business.

"Why don't businesses do their research or conduct evaluations of their clients or customers? I find the bottom line reason is denial. Business owners may not want to hear the truth (good or bad) because they fear they may have to change something about their business. And people fear change, whether it advantages them or not."

Allison emphasizes that market research doesn't have to force you into an uncomfortable box: "I find increasingly often that if business owners position their businesses based on their own unique spirit or passion, they feel more comfortable in their marketing efforts. They derive a deeper and more meaningful experience by integrating their beliefs into their business, and become more successful over time in balancing the growth of the business with their lives. It becomes easier for their clients or customers to understand what they offer, and they begin to attract the customers they desire.

"In other words, instead of trying to be all things to all people—the most common marketing mistake I see among small businesses—the reality is that using your uniqueness in positioning and promoting a business will gain a better market share, and attract the clients with whom you want to conduct business."

Allison Bliss, marketing consultant, Bliss Marketing,
www.blissmarketing.com

true that you can do almost anything in your field of expertise, but people don't buy "anything"; they buy something specific. It's a rare prospect who will agree to meet with you just to share his problems and goals without knowing exactly what you are selling.

A *narrower focus of services* will allow prospects to have a better sense of whether they need you. It will also help them remember who you are. Having people know that you do "something with computers" will not lead to many inquiries or referrals. If they think of you instead as the expert in accounting and financial management software, you could find a place in their card file.

Just as with choosing a target market, don't worry that you are limiting yourself. Once you are in conversation with a prospect, you can propose other services that are within your range of expertise. But you need the narrower focus to get their attention so you can have the conversation in the first place.

| Chapter | 10 |
| --- | --- |

# Closing Sales: When You're Making Appointments But Not Getting Sales

*When you get into a tight place and everything goes against you, till it seems as though you could not hold on a minute longer, never give up then, for that is just the place and time that the tide will turn.*

—Harriet Beecher Stowe

## The Final Frontier

To make your way to this final stage of the universal marketing cycle, you've already done a lot of things right. You've identified good prospects, gotten up the nerve to contact them, and convinced them to meet with you. Getting stuck at this point, after investing a great deal of time and effort, can be really frustrating.

Understand first that some sales can't be made—or at least can't be made now. The vast majority of reasons that a prospect may choose to say no are completely out of your control. In fact, most consultants and professionals find that only one out of three prospects they present to will become a client. This means that at least two out of three are saying no. It's not unusual for this number to be even higher.

Many of the reasons prospects decide not to buy are standard objections you can try to overcome, some of which are covered below under "Making the Sale." Others, however, have more to do with how you are presenting and selling yourself. Since this *is* under your control, some suggestions for improvement follow. First we'll look at issues of credibility and then move on to specific techniques that you can use while carrying out direct contact and follow-up.

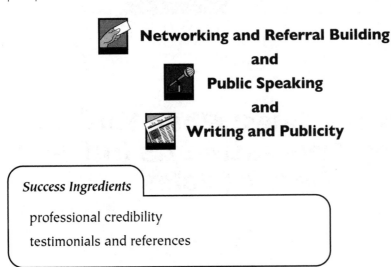

**Networking and Referral Building**

**and**

**Public Speaking**

**and**

**Writing and Publicity**

*Success Ingredients*

professional credibility

testimonials and references

If you find that prospects tend to ask a lot of questions about your background and experience, increasing your *professional credibility* may help to make the sale go through. The marketing strategies of public speaking and writing and publicity are one way to do this. Networking in a professional association (yours or the prospect's) is another. Referral-building activities focused on prominent center-of-influence people is a third.

Take a hard look at your credentials: work experience, formal education, affiliations, and achievements. Based on what you see, would you hire yourself? Without a strong recommendation, prospects may be hesitant to do business with you if your credentials are light.

If it's experience you lack, consider donating your professional services to a community organization. If it's education, it might be time to earn a certificate in your specialty or take a few classes. Find other opportunities to add to your list of accomplishments and affiliations. Teach a class, organize a community or professional event, enter a contest, or seek out an award.

A solid portfolio of *testimonials and references* can also convince prospects of your credibility. Include testimonial quotes on your brochure or a testimonial letter in your marketing kit. The best testimonial letters are written directly to you ("Dear Carl, Thank you so much for the contribution you have made to my company..."), rather than "To Whom It May Concern." Whenever clients tell you how happy they are with the service you are providing, ask if they would be willing to put it in writing. If your service needs to remain confidential, ask for an anonymous testimonial, and identify the client only by job title or city.

Testimonials or your client list are a good idea to include in your marketing materials, but references should be available only on request. You don't want prospects calling your references before they decide to meet with you. Have a list of references ready, though, to offer after your presentation, if they ask. The more current your references are, the better, and be sure all the contact information is up to date.

Whether you let your references know who will be calling them is up to you, but definitely stay in touch with them as long as you continue to give out their names. When choosing who to use as a reference from many possibilities, focus on who can give the best confirmation of your capabilities. If those turn out to be the smaller or more obscure clients, that's okay. You can save the big names to head up your client list.

> Guerrilla Marketing series author Jay Conrad Levinson believes that "the number one factor in influencing purchase decisions is confidence. And the road to confidence is paved with credibility. Having the lowest price, widest selection, or most convenience won't help you much if your prospect doesn't trust you in the first place.
>
> "Absolutely everything you do that is called marketing influences your credibility, and the influence can be positive or negative. Begin with the name of your company, logo, location, business card, brochure, web site, marketing partners, even your attire. You communicate credibility with the people you employ, technology you use, follow-up in which you engage, attention you pay to customers, testimonials you display, and the neatness of your premises.
>
> "You gain credibility with your advertisements, listings in directories, columns and articles you write, and talks you give. You gain it with your newsletter. You gain even more by your support of a noble cause such as the environment. All these little things add up to something called your reputation.
>
> "The most important word in marketing—*commitment*—is something that also fuels your credibility. When people see that you are maintaining consistency in your marketing, they'll assume you're just as committed to quality and service.
>
> "Credibility is not automatic, but it is do-able. Give a seminar. Work hard for a community organization. Nudge customers into referring your business. Word of mouth is omnipotent in the credibility quest. The idea is for you to establish your expertise, your authority, your integrity, your conscientiousness, your professionalism, and therefore—your credibility."
>
> Jay Conrad Levinson, author,
> Guerrilla Marketing International,
> www.gmarketing.com

## Direct Contact and Follow-Up

### Making Better Presentations

*Success Ingredients*

| | |
|---|---|
| better-qualified prospects | presentation skills |
| presentation script | portfolio |
| presentation visuals | leave-behind |

One of the ways to have more presentations turn into sales is to make fewer presentations—fewer, that is, to people who aren't qualified buyers. It's tempting to make a presentation to anyone who will listen, but that just takes up time you could have spent finding *better-qualified prospects*. Review the suggestions in Chapter 9 for developing qualifying questions and finding higher-quality leads and referrals.

Remember that the more people you can get to contact you, instead of your contacting them, the easier your selling task will be. Focusing more effort on professional visibility and generating referrals can help just as much in closing sales as it does in filling the pipeline and getting presentations.

For the presentation itself, you should be prepared with a *presentation script*, whether you will be presenting in person or over the phone. Like a telephone script, this is actually a series of talking points rather than something you memorize and repeat.

#### Presentation Script Outline

1. *Establish rapport.* Introduce yourself, make sure you know whom you are talking to and who else is in the room. When presenting in person, chat about whatever sequence of events got you there or something else you all have in common.

2. *Determine their needs.* Begin by repeating what you already know, and then start asking questions. Your script should include all the questions you must have an answer to in order to write a proposal or close the deal on the spot. Open-ended questions will elicit more information than those that can be answered with a yes or no. Many questions will be specific to your line of business, but here are some typical ones:

   • What is your situation?

   • How important or urgent is it that you solve this problem?

   • What have you already tried?

- When do you need this done, or when were you thinking about getting started?

- What resources do you already have lined up?

- What kind of budget do you have, or what were you expecting to pay?

3. *Explain how you can meet their needs.* Using the information you have just gathered, respond to each problem or goal mentioned by describing how you can help. Use specific examples to illustrate your explanation—for example, "My last client had exactly the same challenge, and what I did for her was…"

4. *Answer their questions.* Find out how you are doing by asking, "What else do you need to know?" Keep asking for and answering questions until they seem satisfied. Address any concerns that come up, one by one. Reassure them that you are the right solution to their problem by responding specifically with how you can help.

5. *Ask for the business.* Don't leave this step out. Even if you know they will want to see a proposal first, are talking to other people, or aren't ready to make a decision, ask anyway. It's the only way you will find out how close you are to making a sale. Whatever they say in response to this question will tell you exactly what you need to resolve before your prospects will buy.

6. *Decide on a next step.* Whether or not you have closed the sale, be absolutely certain that both you and the prospect know what happens next. Is she ready to get started? When? Will there be a contract or purchase order? Who has to sign off on it? Does she need a written proposal? Does she want to check references? Can you call back in a week? If you don't already know, be sure to find out if she is talking to other people before deciding. And be sure to ask if there is anything you can do to help move things forward.

Services are intangible; they can't be seen and touched like a product can. When presenting in person, consider supporting your talking points with some *presentation visuals*. Topics outlined on a flip chart or laptop screen, diagrams, illustrations, and photographs can all help give what you have to say more weight.

Another solution is to bring a *portfolio* of your best work. Artists, designers, and other professionals who work with tangible objects routinely do this, but in fact, anyone can. Your portfolio might include samples of your writing, reports you have prepared, project schedules, program outlines, or action photos of you at work. Going through the portfolio with your prospect or flipping to a certain page as questions arise can establish your expertise.

While a portfolio is something you review with prospects in person, the purpose of a *leave-behind* is to give your prospects a sample of your work they can hang on to or a gift to remember you by. A *leave-behind* that serves as a sample could be a case study, before-and-after photos, or a collection of testimonials. Gift leave-behinds include books, tapes, paper pad holders, coffee cups, or even candy. The idea is to give your prospects a present they will use, and therefore think of you.

Finally, it's possible that your *presentation skills* may also need improvement. For one-on-one presentations, work on your questioning and listening abilities. When you present to groups of people, your speaking skills become more important. Take a workshop, work with a coach, or join a group to get more practice in presenting.

---

"Pay attention to what others say as they say it. Don't formulate your response while they are speaking. Just listen." That's the advice of communications consultant Patricia Haddock, author of nine books and over 400 magazine articles. Here are some of her tips for more powerful presentations:

1. *Use stories and anecdotes to illustrate your points and involve your listeners.* People relate to other people; storytelling captures the imagination and the memory.

2. *Rehearse.* Each time you rehearse your presentation—whether physically or going over it in your mind—you program it into your brain and body. The more familiar you are with the material, the more natural you will sound.

3. *Make continuous eye contact* to draw your listeners to you and keep their attention. Express interest by nodding, making eye contact, and smiling.

4. *Read audience body language* to make sure you are keeping their attention. If you see glazed looks, crossed arms, or blank stares, pick up the pace, move around, ask questions, tell a story, or cut to a key benefit that will wake them up.

5. *Ask open-ended questions* that require more than simple yes or no answers. Require straightforward answers to your questions. Rephrase your question until the person responds appropriately.

6. *Paraphrase* what the other person says, and ask if you are interpreting his or her comments correctly.

7. *Ask for what you want*, and if you hear no, start negotiating.

Patricia Haddock, author and communications consultant,
www.speaking.com/haddock.html

## Making the Sale

*Success Ingredients*

selling script

selling skills

If you're doing your job right, the selling begins before the presentation ends. The moment you begin explaining exactly how your services can solve the prospect's problem, you are selling. So what's the difference between a *selling script* and a presentation script? Not too much. But if you find yourself doing fine until it's time to ask for the business and then start floundering, a better selling script is what you need.

Asking for the business takes many different forms.

### Sample Asking-for-the-Business Questions

"Are you ready to get started?"

"Would you like to schedule an appointment?"

"Shall I draw up a contract?"

"Would you like to sign up?"

"Is my proposal acceptable?"

"Shall I finalize the details?"

"Do we have a deal?"

The most important piece of asking for the business is to ask your closing question and then shut up! Don't talk yourself out of a sale by saying, "Is my proposal acceptable, or is the price too high? You know, we might be able to work out a different arrangement and..." Wait to hear whether your prospect has any objections, and if so, what they are. Even if the silence starts to get uncomfortable, don't speak until your prospect answers you.

The next words out of your prospect's mouth will probably tell you exactly what you need to know to close the sale. And what you are likely to hear is an objection. This doesn't mean you have lost the sale. In fact, it may mean you have made it. "Well, it's a lot of money to spend" is not a real objection; it's probably a statement of fact. An appropriate response might be, "You're right; it's quite an investment. What do you think? Are you ready to take the plunge?"

Real objections, though, need to be overcome—or to put it in language you might like to use with your prospects, they are "considerations that need to be resolved" or "points that need to be handled" in order for the sale to go through. Include in your selling script all the typical objections people in your line of work encounter, and some possible responses to each one.

"We can't afford to spend that much" can be countered with, "What is it costing you not to fix it?" A good response to "I need to think about it" is,

---

"Sales Doctor" Brian Azar claims, "Most salespeople and entrepreneurs don't spend enough time asking prospects about their needs, problems, and concerns. Instead, they just start selling.

"Imagine that you went to the doctor for a checkup, and the doctor said, 'I'm glad you're here today! We've got a special on kidney stone removal—whaddaya say?' And when you answered, 'Doctor, my kidneys are fine,' he or she responded, 'Oh, really? Well, what about a tonsillectomy? Boy, do we do good work, I mean ask anyone! How about it?' You would probably be looking for the door, right?

"Successful salespeople know how to examine their prospects the way a doctor really would. They find the pain, make a diagnosis, write a prescription, and start a treatment plan."

In Brian's book *The Business Survival Guide for the 90's* (Sales Catalyst, 1992), he gives his own prescription for selling: "The Sales Doctor Qualifying Exam." Try asking these simple questions of your prospects and see how they respond:

1. What's your biggest problem in . . . ? (Insert your line of work.)

2. How long have you had it?

3. What have you done to fix it?

4. And that's worked well for you?

5. What is this costing you in terms of time, money, reputation?

6. Do you have a budget set up to solve this problem?

7. Are you the person that makes these decisions?

8. Are you committed to finding a solution to this problem?

Brian Azar, coach, author, and speaker,
The Sales Catalyst, Inc., www.salesdoctor.com

"What are your concerns?" Remember that once you leave the room, you may find yourself back in voice-mail limbo; for that reason, it's wise to make every possible use of this opportunity to deal with your prospect's considerations face-to-face.

If every presentation seems to get bogged down with objections at the end, you are probably asking for the business too soon. Try asking, "What concerns do you have?" before throwing out a closing question. That way you can work to resolve those concerns while you are still in the more comfortable "presenting" phase, and don't yet feel so pressured to "sell."

Learning to do a good job at this kind of verbal dance may require improving your *selling skills*. Books and tapes can help, but significant improvement will take practice. Workshops and other group environments are one way, or you can role-play with a friend or coach. One of the biggest obstacles to successful selling is lack of self-confidence, and that's what practice will help to build.

### Following Up

When you don't make the sale at the time of the presentation, you haven't yet lost it. But if you don't follow up, you probably will. Everyone who has been in business for any length of time has a story about a sale that finally went through 18 months after the presentation or after the eleventh follow-up call. Once you have a prospect on the line who needs you, can pay you, and already knows what you can do for them, don't let go!

---

"Being successful in business is the result of finding enough of the right people, and getting them to buy what they need from you. If you are not asking, you cannot get agreement to provide them with your products or services.

"The only way to meet your goals is to successfully ask for the business as often as you can. Do not worry about who will say no and who will say yes. If you ask enough people, you will definitely get some yeses. When someone turns you down, do not dwell on it. That depletes your energy and your self-esteem, and makes it harder to ask the next time.

"At a recent workshop I was leading, a participant gave me a calendar page that said, 'I did the thing I feared the most. Excuse me while I cheer. Now here I stand a stronger soul and all I've lost is fear.'"

Caterina Rando, Certified Professional and
Personal Coach and speaker,
www.CaterinaR.com

Contact your prospects at regular intervals, using all the methods described in Chapter 8. Be friendly and professional, but be persistent. If they really don't want to hear from you, they will tell you. Until then, keep following up.

## A Final Word About Fear

The moment of truth in a selling conversation is when you ask for the business. As soon as you ask the question, you run the risk of being turned down. The thought of that can be so scary that you stop yourself from asking, and maybe not even consciously. You walk out of the meeting or hang up the phone, and realize that you don't know whether the prospect will buy.

To become successful at selling, you must overcome this last self-imposed obstacle. Try a memory jogger first. When presenting by phone, post a sign bearing your favorite closing question where you can't avoid seeing it. For in-person presentations, you may need to be more subtle. Stick a note inside your calendar, note pad, or card case where you can't miss it.

If you still find yourself choking on the closing question, sneak up on it by asking something more indirect. At the point in the presentation where the prospect has no more questions, ask, "Where are we?" or "What's our next step?" This may give you all the information you need or deliver a positive enough signal that you can safely follow up with a more direct question to see if you have the sale.

Practice asking closing questions with a friend or coach. Trust that the more you ask, the more confident you will become. And remember that the only way to get anything you want in life is to ask for it.

# Index